CW00642575

A LAKE DISTRICT CHRISTMAS

CHRISTMAS PAST

PAGE 3

YULETIDE HAUNTINGS

PAGE 71

SNOW & NATURE

PAGE 87

TRADITIONS

PAGE 117

A LAKE DISTRICT CHRISTMAS

Compiled by Alan Cleaver © 2021.
Edited by David Felton.
Designed by Chapman Design.
Proofread by Rosemary Tyler.

With thanks to James Park, Eva Elliott, Eric Fisher, Ruth Tuer, Joe Ritson, Margaret Crosby and Helen Shipton-Smith.

Printed by Latitude in the EU on woodland-friendly FSC stock.

ISBN 978-1-9998940-8-5.

A catalogue for this book is available from the British Library.

Published October 2021 by Jake Island Ltd, 3 Brunt How, Loughrigg, Cumbria LA22 9HE.

A Lake District Christmas is an Inspired by Lakeland title.

For news and other publications see inspiredbylakeland.co.uk

To get in touch email hello@inspiredbylakeland.co.uk

PART I

CHRISTMAS PAST

CAROL SINGING AT WASDALE

THE historic counties of Cumberland and Westmorland have long traditions of wassailing and carol singing. In pockets of modern-day Cumbria those traditions are kept alive; Dentdale hosts a three-day carol concert each year, and in valleys like Borrowdale and St John's in the Vale, residents still sing door-to-door, with prayers read in each home. This 1913 report from the *Yorkshire Post* chronicles a choral valley wander in winter conditions that deteriorate as the light fades...

'Yorkshire Post', 26 December, 1913.

MY friend the choirmaster used to be annoyed if anyone observed that the surroundings of his abode were a little austere. To him – a man who found the best company in the world in a Beethoven sonata played in his flagged parlour, all by himself, while the guests roared across Irton Fells – the setting of his house was Arcadian.

Yet even in summer, the cottage (it was the cottage where old Will Ritson retired from the patriarchate of Wasdale Head to spend his last days and die) and its whole surroundings – the gnarled crags of Buckbarrow overhead, the mightier cliffs and dark gullies of the Screes in front, Wastwater stretching beyond, and the great fells in the distance – had a high-pitched severity, an absence of all that is soft and sensuous in beauty, but gave full satisfaction only to ascetic taste. And now it was winter; a regular old-fashioned Christmas.

The Screes had disappeared in a wild succession of snow flurries before daylight waned. Opening the front door, we had to shut it by force again, the wind having blown our lantern out, sending the flame in the kitchen lamp flaring up the chimney. Evidently we should have to leave the lantern at home and trust to the fitful light of the moon on our way to the trysting place with the choristers on Wasdale Green.

The broken and furrowed surface of the Moor was now strangely even. The fairest and most seductive sheets of white were snow-wreaths, and spangles of moonlight on the descending track marked many a frozen rivulet, where the feet slithered or broke through into pools and bog. Ahead, at intervals, Irton Fells rose to the sky like a snow cloud – lustrous above, shadowy below.

We came out of the wood by the church to the May-pole on Wasdale Green. It was chiefly the junior choristers who had gathered there. On Christmas Eve the whole choir had done the round of the three big houses and the outer farms, leaving the inner ring of cottages about the village green for a second performance. And now the basses and tenors had betrayed us, so that we three or four, with the vicar and the choir master, had to make shift to furnish harmony to the boys. Even the blind fiddler had succumbed to the weather, and the only instrumental aid forthcoming was a tuning fork that pitched the key.

There is not much poetry in carol singing nowadays. Even in Cumberland villages, where it is still something more than a periodical mendicancy, it drops too often into drunkenness and horseplay. Our Wasdale carols were an effort to revive the ancient spirit of Yule; the sentiment of the village as a family circle, where once a year at least, all might forget parochial and sectarian differences and join in one immemorial act of worship and human kindness. For so ran our wassail song:

> We are not daily beggars
> That beg from door to door;
> But we are neighbours' children
> Whom you have met before.
>
> Love and joy come to you
> And to your wassail too,
> And God bless you, and send you
> A happy New Year.

Only at one door was there any mistaking of our motives, and some money offered and refused. The following verse had been carefully omitted:

> We have made a little purse
> Made of ratching leather skin,
> We want some of your small change
> To line it well within.

From the vicarage garden, where the strains of 'The First Nowell' rose angelically to the winds of heaven, we moved across the farm-house hard by the church, and thence to the nearest cottages. Our lanterns were alight now, not, however, to show us the way, but to light up our song books – though the wind pursuing us into corners made our science look rather foolish.

Not to the dark fronts of the houses did we go, but to the backs, where lighted windows gave a view of the kitchen, with the family perhaps at supper. Sometimes offers of cakes and oranges delayed the efforts of the trebles. Time and place may put poetry into the simple verse, and at the doors of these humble cots it did not sound like doggerel when we sang:

> God bless the master of this house,
> Likewise the mistress too,
> And all the little children
> That round the table go.

Plenty of local colour marked our rendering of 'Good King Wenceslas': a snow-squall had blotted out the moon, and blasts of snow-dust from the drifts were tangibly being reinforced by new fall. Very feelingly the lads (one or two with failing voices) carolled:

> Mark my footsteps, my good page,
> Tread thou in them boldly;
> Thou shalt find the winter's rage
> Freeze thy blood less coldly.
>
> In his master's steps he trod
> Where the snow lay dinted,
> Heat was in the very sod
> Which the saint had printed.

But as the storm continued, the cottagers were less eager to open theit doors and let in the chilly draught; and certain trebles mysteriously vanished, their homes taking toll of them as we passed by. The flight of the valiant also having still further marred our sweet concert, we dismissed the small remnant, and took our way through the driving snow homeward across the Moor. ❄

NOTES ON CHRISTMAS

MANY writers record the Christmas traditions of their time and childhood. John Briggs, former editor of *The Westmorland Gazette* – a paper still thriving today – penned his memories of the season in 1825, giving an insight into a Westmorland Christmas two centuries ago.

'The Remains of John Briggs', John Briggs, 1825.

RELICS of the Christmas feasts, to a greater or less degree, remain in all parts of the country. In most places the ancient hospitality, though expatriated from the dwellings of the rich, was permitted to creep into the servants hall on Christmas Eve. All the labourers and mechanics of the neighbourhood paid their annual visit to the kitchens of those houses, where they could produce a claim, however weak, such as: ever having worked for the master; having opened a gate for him when hunting; being the son of some person who had been servant to the master's father; being 32nd cousin to one of the servants; being very kind with some person who was very intimate with the shoeblack's assistant... or in fact, any cause which would get the visitor within the door at a time when all was gaiety, and no particular attention paid to the bearing of the guests.

Then came out the two gallon copper, foaming with Brown October*, that 'drank divinely'. The full horns were handed round with cheerfulness, and "A merry Christmas, and a happy New Year" invoked upon the heads of all the family, even down to the favourite lapdog, whose treble bark cheered the lone hours of the housekeeper, while the butler attended his master to London. Many was the tale and smutty jest which circled round the old kitchen on this joyous night. And as many of the stories had not been told since the last Christmas Eve, the company was ready to hail them with fresh cheerings.

Early in the morning, every old man who could 'rub the hair of the horse over the bowels of the cat'† wandered from house to house, in company with some neighbour, whose Stentorian voice was best calculated to 'break the bands of sleep asunder'. The honest inhabitants of Westmorland cottages were agreeably roused from their dreams of mince pies and 'three card lant' (as loo is called in this country‡), by the elegant air of 'Hunsup through the wood', and the homely salute of: "Good morning, John Dixon, good morning, Betty Dixon, and all the rest of your family; I wish you a merry Christmas, and a happy new year." It often happened that while the husband was gone to 'open Christmas' in the great man's kitchen, the good wife was plucking geese and preparing sweet pies at home; so that the fiddlers were often invited in to the first taste of Christmas cheer in these their nocturnal visitings; and as daylight began to glent in the sky, the two minstrels might be seen toddling towards home with their 'skins fu'.

In such places as could boast a set of bells, the brazen music from the church steeple announced that it was Christmas Day. At the joyous sound, all the boys within hearing of them quitted their beds to load the kitchen hearth with a huge fire, the most conspicuous object of which was a huge piece of wood – pompously denominated the 'Christmas stock'.

In farm houses, the master's first duty was to compliment every cow with a sheaf of corn, and then return to broach the 'Christmas drink'. This done, the boys and young men sallied out into the villages, singing this very elegant piece of poetry, which Sir Walter Scott has overlooked in collecting his relics:

> Get up auld wives
> An 'byak your pies
> A Kersmas Day in the morning.

The enunciation of this minstrelsy generally procured a good appetite for tea and hot buns which awaited their return. It is only, however, within recent times that the male part of these families has allowed everyone to share in a full breakfast: a basin of milk porridge and in some places a basin of sweet broth preceded the tea, one cup of which was considered a great treat. The sweet broth was made from the mutton which had been boiled for the mince pies, and was seasoned with sugar, raisins, currants, cloves, &c.

The breakfast being over, generally by daybreak, the boys procured a quantity of yew, box, laurel and other evergreens, with which the girls decorated the windows. The clerk of the church or chapel took care to adorn the candlesticks, windows, pulpit and in some places even the pews in a similar manner. In Westmorland, box and yew were and are considered indispensable, but in some parts of Lancashire, where no yew grows and wild box is not cultivated, and the plant stonecrop (*Sedum reflexum*) is nourished in flowerpots, spruce or Scotch fir is used as an evergreen for adorning both houses and places of worship.

The morning work done, the young men, dressed in their 'Sunday duds', went into the fields with guns, for Christmas Day was a great day for field sports. Even long after the introduction of the game laws, the more wealthy part of the community connived at this practice, and allowed their more indigent brethren to enjoy the sports of the field for one day out of 365. We believe that in many of the less civilised parts of the country, particularly in Lancashire and Cumberland, this custom is not yet abolished. Where the privilege was denied, a custom obtained of shooting at a target upon a barn door for a tea kettle or other trifling prize. Where the observances of religion are more strictly enforced, that sport is also denied, and the shooting takes place on the following day; and a sober game of whist or loo fills the tedium of Christmas Day in the afternoon, so impossible it is to compel people to be virtuous.

The custom of giving Christmas boxes has been long laid aside. And little of that feasting which took place at Christmas now remains. In some of the more retired parts of the country, however, the ancient custom continues. Ale, brewed expressly for the season and uncommonly strong, called 'Christmas drink', is prepared for the occasion.

A large quantity of mince pies are hung up in baskets over the dairy, and every visitor – whether friend or stranger – is invited in and treated with a pot of beer and a mince pie.

Dances are made at the village inns and card parties for buns or pears take place at the farm houses. Sometimes these card parties are for a goose, a leg of mutton – or a whole sheep. ❄

* *Brown October – An ale.*
† *'Rub the hair of the horse over the bowels of the cat' – To play the violin or fiddle.*
‡ *Loo was a popular card game, like whist. It was often known as three-card lant in the north country.*

BORROWDALE IN THE OLD TIME

SARAH Yewdale was known as the Queen of Borrowdale, having lived in the Lakeland valley her whole life. Memories of Christmases past – of Yule logs, dances and long frosty winters – were recorded before her death at the grand age of 101 in 1869.

'Borrowdale in the Old Time', Rev. James Dixon, 1869.

Christmas was Christmas then, a thing the folk of the old time enjoyed a lot more than they do now, and when they were always far more friendly with one and another. For a week before Christmas, everybody began to be busy, and for all that week there was such 'scrows'*, with killing of sheep and splitting of woods, and baking of pies as never was seen. Then old Yule Iben – a gay great log – was put on the back of the fire and the barrel was tapped and all tidied up, and the fiddler would come and a few great fellows with him, and if folk weren't going to bed there would be a dance, and away again.

It was a regular thing to brew in October for Christmas. Everybody did so, both rich and poor, and some brewed at same time as clippen. But when Christmas was once fairly set in, we did nowt but feast and dance and play at cards 'til Candlemas. In them days we always had a fiddler in the Dale and there was never a feast but there was a dance. What barn! You fairly ran through yourself at such times – night after night feasting and dancing 'til one would go off to sleep the next day among one's work. But there was no pride and difference among us then; servants and statesmans' sons and daughters were all alike, as well they must…

The wad mines† were open mainly in summertime, for folk in them days didn't do much work in winter, for you see winters were nowt like what they are now. From November 'til Candlemas we had nothing but frost and snow, and very seldom did snow get off the fell tops before midsummer. I can remember when it was a very common thing to have to take geavelick⁑ to break the ice in the beck for cows to drink. What, I can remember where Darran‡ was once frozen over for 13 weeks. But we have nowt o' that swort now, nor such fine summers. We've nowt but rain and such now; snell• weather that I cannot put my head to today without getting cold. ❄

* *Scrow – Cumbrian dialect for disorder or confusion.*
† *Wad mines – Borrowdale was historically a lucrative source of wad (graphite).*
⁑ *Geavelick – An iron bar.*
‡ *Darran – Dialect pronunciation of Derwent.*
• *Snell – Keen, sharp.*

DOROTHY'S CHRISTMAS DIARIES

FOR recollections of Yules past, one of the most evocative narrators is Dorothy Wordsworth, and the *Grasmere Journal* she maintained between May 1800 and January 1803. In the following extracts we trace the Wordsworth family through the Christmas of 1801 – a time of long walks, varied company... and plenty of Chaucer.

'Journals of Dorothy Wordsworth', Ed. William Knight, 1897.

WEDNESDAY Morning, 9 December, 1801. Mary and I* walked into Easedale... We had intended gathering mosses, and for that purpose we turned into the green lane behind the tailor's, but it was too dark to see the mosses. The river came galloping past the church, as fast as it could come; and when we got into Easedale we saw Churn Milk Force, like a broad stream of snow at the little footbridge. We stopped to look at the company of rivers, which came hurrying down the vale, this way and that. It was a valley of streams and islands, with that great waterfall at the head, and lesser falls in different parts of the mountains, coming down to these rivers. We could hear the sound of the lesser falls, but we could not see them. We walked backwards and forwards till all distant objects, except the white shape of the waterfall and the lines of the mountains, were gone. We had the crescent moon when we went out, and at our return there were a few stars that shone dimly, but it was a grey cloudy night.

Saturday, 12 December: Snow upon the ground... All looked cheerful and bright. Helm Crag rose very bold and craggy, a Being by itself, and behind it was the large ridge of mountain, smooth as marble and snow white. All the mountains looked like solid stone on our left going from Grasmere, i.e. White Moss and Nab Scar. The snow hid all the grass, and all signs of vegetation, and the rocks showed themselves boldly everywhere, and seemed more stony than rock or stone. The birches on the crags were beautiful, red brown and glittering; the ashes glittering spears with their upright stems.

I came home first. They walked too slow for me. William [Wm.] went to look at Langdale Pikes. We had a sweet invigorating walk... We played at cards. Sat up late. The moon shone upon the waters below Silver How, and above it hung, combining with Silver How on one side, a bowl-shaped moon, the curve downwards, the white fields, glittering roof of Thomas Ashburner's house, the dark yew tree, the white fields gay and beautiful. Wm. lay with his curtains open that he might see it.

Thursday, 17 December: Snow in the night and still snowing... Ambleside looked excessively beautiful as we came out – like a village in another country; and the light cheerful mountains were seen, in the long distance, as bright and as clear as at mid-day, with the blue sky above them. We heard waterfowl calling out by the lake side. Jupiter was glorious above the Ambleside hills, and one large star hung over the corner of the hills on the opposite side of Rydal water.

Sunday, 20 December: It snowed all day. It was a very deep snow. The brooms were very beautiful – arched feathers with wiry stalks pointed to the end, smaller and smaller. They waved gently with the weight of the snow.

Monday, 21 December: Being the shortest day, Mary walked to Ambleside for letters. It was a wearisome walk, for the snow lay deep upon the roads and it was beginning to thaw. I stayed at home. Wm. sat beside me and read 'The Pedlar'†. He was in good spirits, and full of hope of what he should do with it. He went to meet Mary, and they brought four letters – two from Coleridge, one from Sara, and one from France. Coleridge's were melancholy letters. He had been very ill. We were made very unhappy. Wm. wrote to him and directed the letter into Somersetshire. I finished it after tea. In the afternoon Mary and I ironed.

Tuesday, 22 December: Wm. composed a few lines of 'The Pedlar'. We... went down the White Moss. We stopped a long time in going to watch a little bird with a salmon-coloured breast, a white cross or 'T' upon its wings, and a brownish back with faint stripes... It began to pick upon the road at the distance of four yards from us, and advanced nearer and nearer till it came within the length of Wm.'s stick, without any apparent fear of us.

As we came up the White Moss, we met an old man, who I saw was a beggar by his two bags hanging over his shoulder; but, from half laziness, half indifference, and wanting to try him – if he would speak – I let him pass. He said nothing, and my heart smote me. I turned back, and said, "You are begging?" "Ay," says he. I gave him something. William, judging from his appearance, joined in, "I suppose you were a sailor?" "Ay," he replied, "I have been 57 years at sea, 12 of them on board a man-of-war under Sir Hugh Palmer." "Why have you not a pension?" "I have no pension; I could have got into Greenwich hospital, but all my officers are dead."

He was 75 years of age, had a freshish colour in his cheeks, grey hair, a decent hat with a binding round the edge, the hat worn brown and glossy, his shoes were small thin shoes low in the quarters – pretty good. They had belonged to a gentleman. His coat was frock shaped, coming over his thighs. It had been joined up at the seams behind with paler blue, to let it out, and there were three bell-shaped patches of darker blue behind, where the buttons had been. His breeches were either of fustian, or grey cloth, with strings hanging down, whole and tight. He had a checked shirt on, and a small coloured handkerchief tied round his neck. His bags were hung over each shoulder, and lay on each side of him, below

his breast. One was brownish, and of coarse stuff; the other was white with meal on the outside. His blue waistcoat was whitened with meal.

I found Mary at home in her riding-habit, all her clothes being put up. We stopped to look at the stone seat at the top of the hill. There was a white cushion upon it, round at the edge like a cushion, and the rock behind looked soft as velvet, of a vivid green, and so tempting! The snow, too, looked as soft as a down cushion, a young foxglove, like a star, in the centre. There were a few green lichens about it, and a few withered brackens of fern here and there upon the ground near. All else was a thick snow; no footmark to it, nor the foot of a sheep. We sate snugly round the fire. I read to them the Tale of Constance and the Syrian monarch in 'The Man of Lawe's Tale', also some of 'The Prologue'.

Wednesday, 23 December: Mary wrote out the Tales from Chaucer for Coleridge. William worked at 'The Ruined Cottage' and made himself very ill... A broken soldier came to beg in the morning; afterwards a tall woman dressed somewhat in a tawdry style, with a long checked muslin apron, a beaver hat, and throughout what are called good clothes. Her daughter had gone before, with a soldier and his wife. She had buried her husband at Whitehaven, and was going back into Cheshire.

Thursday, 24 December: Still a thaw. Wm., Mary, and I sat comfortably round the fire in the evening and read Chaucer. Thoughts of last year. I took out my old Journal.

Friday, 25 December: Christmas Day⁑. We received a letter from Coleridge. His letter made us uneasy about him. I was glad I was not by myself when I received it.

Saturday, 26 December: We walked to Rydal. Grasmere Lake a beautiful image of stillness – clear as glass, reflecting all things. The wind was up, and the waters sounding. The lake of a rich purple, the fields a soft yellow, the island yellowish-green, the copses red-brown, the mountains purple; the church and buildings – how quiet they were! After tea we sate by the fire comfortably. I read aloud 'The Miller's Tale'. Wrote to Coleridge... Wm. wrote part of the poem to Coleridge.

Monday, 28 December: William, Mary and I set off on foot to Keswick. We carried some cold mutton in our pockets and dined at John Stanley's‡, where they were making Christmas pies. The sun shone, but it was coldish. We parted from Wm. upon the Raise. He joined us opposite Sara's rock•. He was busy in composition, and sate down upon the wall. We did not see him again till we arrived at John Stanley's. There we roasted apples in the room. After we had left John Stanley's, Wm. discovered that he had lost his gloves. He turned back, but they were gone.

We reached Greta Hall at about half past 5 o'clock, the children and Mrs. Coleridge well. After tea, message came from Wilkinson, who had passed us on the road, inviting Wm. to sup at The Oak. He went. Met a young man (a predestined Marquis) called Johnston. He spoke to him familiarly of the 'Lyrical Ballads'. He had seen a copy presented by the Queen to Mrs. Harcourt. Said he saw them everywhere, and wondered they did not sell. We all went weary to bed...

Tuesday, 29 December: A fine morning – a thin fog upon the hills which soon disappeared. The sun shone. Wilkinson went with us to the top of the hill. We turned out of the road at the second mile stone and passed a pretty cluster of houses at the foot of St. John's Vale. The houses were among tall trees, partly of Scotch fir, and some naked forest trees. We crossed a bridge just below these houses, and the river winded sweetly along the meadows.

Our road soon led us along the sides of dreary bare hills, but we had a glorious prospect to the left of Saddleback, half-way covered with snow, and underneath the comfortable white houses and the village of Threlkeld. These houses and the village want trees about them. Skiddaw was behind us, and dear Coleridge's desert home. As we ascended the hills it grew very cold and slippery. Luckily, the wind was at our backs and helped us on. A sharp hail shower gathered at the head of Martindale, and the view upwards was very grand – wild cottages, seen through the hurrying hail-shower. The wind drove, and eddied about and about, and the hills looked large and swelling through the storm. We thought of Coleridge. O! the bonny nooks, and windings, and curlings of the beck, down at the bottom of the steep green mossy banks. We dined at the public-house on porridge, with a second course of Christmas pies. We were well received by the landlady, and her little Jewish daughter was glad to see us again. The husband a very handsome man...

The landlord went about a-mile-and-a-half with us to put us in the right way. The road was often very slippery, the wind high, and it was nearly dark before we got into the right road. I was often obliged to crawl on all fours, and Mary fell many a time. A stout young man whom we met on the hills... very kindly set us into the right road, and we inquired again near some houses and were directed by a miserable, poverty-struck, looking woman, who had been fetching water, to go down a miry lane. We soon got into the main road and reached Mr. Clarkson's at tea time.

Mary H. spent the next day with us, and we walked on Dunmallet before dinner, but it snowed a little. The day following, being New Year's Eve, we accompanied Mary to Howtown Bridge. ❄

* *Mary Wordsworth was William Wordsworth's wife, and Dorothy Wordsworth William's sister.*

† *'The Pedlar' was an early poem of William Wordsworth's.*

⁑ *Dorothy Wordsworth's birthday was Christmas Day – though it is not a day she marked with great celebration. The marking of birthdays is a relatively modern tradition.*

‡ *John Stanley was landlord of the King's Head in Keswick.*

• *Sara's rock – also known as The Rock of Names – was the name given by Wordsworth to a rock he and his friends carved their initials on. Sara's rock has been moved from its original location near Wythburn, and part of it now lies in the garden of Dove Cottage. Sara (Hutchinson) was William's sister-in-law.*

FROM COTTAGE TO PALACE

ETHEL Fisher died in 2018 at the age of 90, having lived in Seaton for most of her life. Ethel was a champion for Cumbria and its history, writing various books in local dialect, and she was awarded the MBE for her services to the Seaton community. This extract from her book, *From Cottage to Palace*, recalls her memories of Christmas in the 1930s.

'From Cottage to Palace', Ethel Fisher, 2004.

AFTER Guy Fawkes Night... roll on Christmas. Always a great time, the excitement started early in December when Dad brought home a berried holly bush from nearby Aigle Ghyll Woods and suspended it from the ceiling. I suppose there wouldn't have been enough room for it on the floor with six youngsters tearing around. Coloured baubles and strings of silver tinsel decorated the tree. These were kept in a shoe box on the pantry shelf during the year, so that new ones hadn't to be bought every Christmas. Paper streamers in the shape of multi-coloured fans were strung across the ceiling, intermingled with paper chains and Chinese lanterns, which we made at school every year. Mam made lovely butterflies using wooden clothes pegs and brightly-coloured crêpe paper. These were pinned onto the curtains.

The week before Christmas was a busy time for us. Mam taught us that if we cleaned, scrubbed and polished our toys from previous years – dolls, prams, engines, farm-yards, boards and easels – and left them out on show over Christmas Eve, Father Christmas would see we had cared for them over the year and would be encouraged to leave us more. Looking back, this idea would serve a double purpose: to get our toys cleaned up and to keep us occupied during the last few hectic days before Santa came, when we would no doubt be too excited to either sit and read or play quietly. It would give her breathing space to get the Christmas baking done, and all the other extra jobs the time of year entailed.

Dad, too, was kept busy, tidying up our old family rocking horse each Christmas, repainting it and fitting a new mane and tail made from sheep's wool. This was also purposely done and left on show so that Father Christmas would take note.

We saved any pennies and half-pennies we got in the few weeks before Christmas. These were put on the mantelpiece in little individual piles on Christmas Eve, alongside the mince pie and glass of wine which we left for Father Christmas. Needless to say, all had disappeared when we awoke the following morning to find our stockings filled, mainly with useful things like hand-knitted gloves and socks, and always an orange, a few nuts and one or two new toys. There was nothing elaborate – colouring books and crayons were always evident – I suppose because they kept us quiet for a while, and we certainly liked them. For many years I played schools with my dolls using a small board and easel I'd been bought at Christmas; it was one of my favourite toys.

Dinner on Christmas Day was a rowdy affair, with everyone demanding a leg off the cock chicken Mam had cooked. Dad reminded us every year that it was a chicken he was carving – not a centipede! We didn't get a lot of sweets, but each one of us had a small sugar pig with a coloured woolly tail. These were strung across the kitchen to be eaten on Boxing Day.

Yes, Christmas times were greatly enjoyed and passed all too quickly. Immediately after Boxing Day the decorations were taken down and the holly burnt on the kitchen fire. What a lovely smell it made whilst burning.

My younger sister and I usually attended two socials between Christmas and New Year. One was at our local Sunday School, where we all got a new handkerchief and some sweets, the evening ending with a 'scram alley', where monkey nuts were thrown by the handful across the hall floor, and the winner was the child who picked most up after the whistle blew. The other social was held at the Palace Ballroom in Maryport, now the Civic Hall. This was an annual treat from a maiden aunt, who was allowed to sit in the gallery and watch the proceedings. I'm sure she enjoyed the occasion far more than we did!

So ended our year – and the older we got, the faster the years flew by. ❄

A CHRISTMAS SHOPPING LIST, 1721

TODAY Christmas shopping can be frantic – even if we do it online. These extracts, from a Troutbeck account book, paint a picture of the housekeeping of past times, detailing "the good housewife's preparations for the jollifications at Christmas". Our author explains that "poultry and geese were kept in pens till about the end of February, and at Christmas, pies were baked, made of flour and containing meat, generally goose or mutton, or sweetmeats." Preparations for the big day began on 14 December...

'A Westmorland Village; The story of the old homesteads and 'statesman' families of Troutbeck by Windermere', S. H. Scott, 1904.

NOTHING affords a better illustration of the housekeeping of past times than extracts which may be made from an old account book. The items contained in a Troutbeck diary begun in 1721 are very interesting from this point of view. On one page we find the good housewife's preparations for the jollifications at Christmas:

14 December, 1721

ITEM	AMOUNT	COST
Wheat flour	1 peck	3 shillings [s]
Currants and raisins	4lbs	2s
Nutmegs	1oz	9 pence [d]
Aniseed	¼oz	3d
A sugar loaf	5lbs at 9½d	3s 11½d

ITEM	AMOUNT	COST
Figs	1lb	4d
Prunes	1lb	4d
Treacle	3lbs	7d
Brown sugar	4lbs at 5d	1s 8d
Brown natural sugar	6lb at 4¾d	2s 1½d
Powdered sugar	6lbs at 7d	3s 6d
December 19		
Gingerbread	4lbs	1s
To Peggy for butter	4lbs	1s
A cheese sent to Ben: per Mr. Speight		2s
December 21		
Brandy	2½ gallons	15s 0d
To Mr. Alderman Dodgson for 2 gallons of rum		11s 6d
December 22		
Off Mary Knott: 5 pints of cherry brandy		2s 6d
Spirit of wine	1 pint	9d
A wax candle	1lb	2s 0d
Frankincense		2d

THE CHRISTMAS MAIL

THE arrival of Christmas mail – and the season's news and greetings contained therein – was always eagerly anticipated. But the journey of the mail cart on the roads of yesteryear was often an arduous one, especially when the snows came.

'The Christmas Mail', W. T. Palmer, December 1929.

THE mail cart was an institution which varied from a real turn-out with three or four horses (and a twanging bugle which warned users of the narrow lanes to get out of the way quickly), to an aged donkey, which used to stand meditative on the railway station while the old owner-driver went in search of a possible postal-package for some village.

At Christmas... the whisky flowed like water round the postman who brought up the mail, be the day frosty or dirty or merely unpleasant. One has known the Christmas mail come through the pass on a day of raging snow, with drifts among the wheels, extra horses, and a postillion on the leaders. It was such a morning that old Jim alluded to when we were driving through the dark morning to Grasmere: "They tells me that motors are going to be put on this job; but, believe me, it can't be done. Them hosses can either see, or hear, or smell their way in the worst storm as ever blew, and they never swerve a foot from their place on the road."

Many a Christmas mail had old Jim brought to the village, and the way his mail slipped about the ice-bound roads was something to remember. In these days, racing motorcyclists dash round dirt tracks and skid their corners; wonders never cease, but old Jim and other drivers of the Christmas mails half-a-century or more ago did the same thing, and a plunging horse-team and hummocky roads added sensation. Old Jim, who drove until the last horse-mail in Westmorland was swept away by the motor van, was a link with the great coach drivers of the past.

In 1754 a Manchester firm undertook that their conveyance would reach London in four-and-a-half days. It was not until 1784 that the Christmas mail, such as it was, went by coach instead of by postboys and mounted couriers. In August of that year the 'New Mail Diligence' stagecoach ran from London to Bath between eight at night and daylight next morning; a coachman who received his mails late was expected to make up lost time on his stage. The Edinburgh mail ultimately ran its 400 miles to London in 40 hours, and some of the coaches became so punctual that the cottagers and villagers set their clocks by the minute of their passing. The Glasgow–Carlisle coach averaged 11-and-a-half miles per hour.

Storm often delayed, but it rarely stopped the Christmas mail altogether. The great crimson conveyance, with its powerful lamps, its good teams and skilful driver, kept going at all costs. The terrific storm of December 1836 tested the road users terribly; for days on end London was isolated from the provinces.

The guards had a fierce time of it, for the mails were their personal concern; if the coach ditched or became stuck in a drift, the guard had to take a horse and ride on with the mail bags into the storm. Sometimes this meant loss of life; one has stood on the old Edinburgh turnpike near Moffatt and looked up the ladder-like ascent of the moor where the guard and driver of the Dumfries and Edinburgh Royal Mail coach died in 1831. They had taken the mail bags on their own shoulders after the road was drifted too much for wheels, and went forward on foot until they were overwhelmed. ❄

THE LONELIEST CHRISTMAS ROUND

In the not–so–distant days before the familiar red van, rural postmen trudged for hours, sometimes through snow, to reach remote farmhouses and bring Christmas cheer. Spare a thought for this reporter from *The Penrith Herald,* assigned to accompany a postie on the toughest of rural rounds – a six–hour tramp among the fells west of Shap.

'The Penrith Herald', 29 December, 1956.

IN cities, towns and villages on every weekday the letterbox in the front door of millions of houses clinks as the morning mail is pressed through by the postman. The letters patter onto the mat, and the man who has delivered them passes on – an unseen caller whose visits are very much taken for granted. But on some remote country rounds, the postman is a particularly welcome visitor, providing the householders' only link with the outside world. His daily call is more than a mere formality; rather it is a friendly occasion in the lonely routine of people who would otherwise go for days without seeing or speaking to anyone. This is the story of one such round – of a postman's 15-mile walk each day to deliver letters and parcels to the isolated houses and farms in Swindale and Wet Sleddale, two bleak valleys on top of Shap Fell. To obtain a first-hand account of his day's work and see the mail to its destination, a *Herald* reporter set out one morning this month with Mr Jim Eland, Southwaite Green Mill, Eamont Bridge, who covers that area, and here he records his impressions of the six-hour trek over the fells.

After preliminary consultation with the Head Postmaster at Penrith, Mr H. Williams, and several of his staff, I arrived at the Penrith sorting office at 6.15am on the appointed day.

My instructions were to report to Inspector T. Wilson, and this I did complete with heavy walking boots, and clad – as I thought – to withstand the worst any weather could bring.

The Shap mail is sorted in the office by four postmen, and at 8am Mr Eland and I left on foot to begin the rural round. After visits to houses and farms at the south end of the village, our first outlying port of call was High Buildings Farm, where Mr E. W. Bindloss and his housekeeper, Miss Irving, were there to wish us "Good morning". How welcome the postman is was shown by the greeting he received here and at every other house on the route. Mr Bindloss is probably one of the best-known sheep breeders in the two counties; he has many hundreds of acres of fell-grazing in the Shap district.

From High Buildings we set off for Shap Abbey, which at the present time is in the hands of the Ministry of Works, who are renovating and repairing the crumbling stone. Across a field we walked, and then began our 'assault' on the fells. The soaking turf underfoot made parts of the journey very difficult, and to make matters worse there was a strong wind, making our progress at times very slow.

The next farm at which we called was Tailbert, occupied by Mr and Mrs N. Harrison, who have only been there a short time. Tailbert Head is just across the field, and here I met Miss Mary Burgess. Over 60 years old, but as young in heart and mind as anyone half her age, Miss Burgess was born at High Farm, Langwathby.

She has lived at Tailbert Head for 21 years and has been in Shap village only once in all that time. That was three years ago after the death of her mother, who had to be taken into Shap by tractor to be buried because no other vehicle could reach the farm.

Educated in Penrith by the late Mr James Briggs, Miss Burgess is well-read and takes a keen interest in the affairs of the outside world, with most of her spare time being spent reading. She has not even the wireless for entertainment! She prefers the quietude of her lovely home to life in a village – even though the only people she gets a chance to speak to are the postman on his daily round and the grocer and coal merchant when they call once a month.

After bidding our farewells to Miss Burgess, we set off once more to Swindale Foot Farm, where we had a 30-minute rest for a meal, with Mr and Mrs A. Buckle as our hosts. Many postmen serving isolated areas have their meals 'on the job' in this way. Mr Buckle and his family have spent many years in Swindale and have a wide knowledge of the district and its inhabitants. Of much interest to them just now is the new water undertaking in the valley, where Manchester Corporation are building a tunnel to take water from Swindale into Haweswater. Outside the door of Mr Buckle's home, the noise of cement mixers, dumpers, excavators and compression engines has become a part of the everyday life of the household.

Leaving Swindale Foot after our rest, we walked on up the valley along a pathway of rock chippings. Next we came to Truss Gap Farm, occupied by Mr Buckle's two sons, Robert and Nelson, and Jim pointed out to me the 'postman's path'* which he takes some days to shorten his journey. This 'path' is marked on the fell-top by stakes in the ground because of the treacherous nature of the marshy land in misty weather.

After leaving Truss Gap we came upon a dilapidated building which I was told was the old chapel and school built to serve the residents of Swindale. Many years ago there used to be several more farms in the valley, and even the old Swindale public house is still standing – though now converted into farm buildings.

The last farm in Swindale valley is appropriately called Swindale Head, and here I met Mr and Mrs Lionel Atkinson, who have lived there for about a year. After chatting for several minutes we set off on the climb over Mosedale into Wet Sleddale.

After climbing for about quarter-of-an-hour, we rested to admire the view spread out before us. Down in the valley bottom, Lionel Atkinson was in a field with his three sheepdogs, gathering up his flock, and it was a wonderful sight to look down upon the columns of sheep keeping to their 'trods' in their slow walk before the dogs.

A strong wind had suddenly risen, and the shape of the valley head was turning its blast into strong eddies, whipping spray off the fell beck and threatening to blow us from our lofty perch. To our right, Swindale Beck was tumbling over rocks and cascading in miniature waterfalls in its descent to the valley bottom. Across the valley we could see the fell walls in their jigsaw pattern as they ran up and down the steep fell sides; Jim told me a local legend had it that the stone for these walls was carried by pack mule several miles across the fell from an old now-disused quarry in Mosedale.

It was time to carry on once more, and we turned our backs on the scene and began our climb again. Over the top we went, and by now the wind and rain were at their worst. After tramping for about a mile, Jim said we would soon be able to see the cottage at Mosedale Head, occupied only for six weeks in the year – during November and December – by Bill Benson, shepherd for Mr Bindloss. The cottage, which is situated 1,800 feet above sea level and is over three miles from the nearest habitation, is used by Mr Benson while gathering up the tups for tupping time. When we were within hailing distance of the cottage, I spotted him about half-a-mile away, setting off on his day's work.

By whistling and shouting we eventually managed to attract Mr Benson's attention, and then walked towards each other across the fell and stopped for a chat. The wind was now blowing with almost gale force, and across the wide expanse of rolling fell country the higher peaks were invisible under a shroud of mist. The rain, too, blotted out parts of the scenery, and the three of us often had difficulty in making ourselves heard above the howling wind.

A shepherd who lived there many years ago, a man by the name of Sutherland, is reputed to have had two children who never saw beyond the fells until they were five years old, when they were taken to school in Shap. It is said that when they saw their first tree they were so frightened that they wanted to return to Mosedale!

On our way over from Mosedale to Wet Sleddale we followed an old road which was made for the use of cars to take stone from the quarry at the head of Mosedale. Now the ruts are so deep that it would be impossible to take any vehicle along it. We walked for over three miles down the fell side, with the wind and rain beating on us relentlessly from behind until we arrived at Sleddale Hall†, the furthest point up the valley to which a car can get, which was our last port of call.

Finally came the two-mile walk back to Shap, with our steps getting faster as we contemplated the pleasing prospect of the warm bath and hot meal that awaited us back home!

During his five years on this round, Jim Eland has had some interesting experiences and I enjoyed listening to his tales, which helped to while away the time as we made our way over the fell tracks. His unpleasant experiences are many, of course, being chiefly caused by the weather. Once he was stuck in a snowdrift and it took him over three-quarters-of-an-hour to get out. The little gullies in the fell side all fill up in a snowstorm, and it is difficult to remember where they are. It was into one of these that he unknowingly stepped on the occasion mentioned.

But the job has compensations. A great nature lover, Jim is particularly interested in birds – he pointed out to me a hole in a tree where he once saw a green woodpecker at work – yet perhaps the greatest source of satisfaction in his arduous daily round, over rough country and in all weathers, is the warmth of the welcome he receives wherever he goes. That in itself must indeed make it all seem well worthwhile. ❄

** It is still possible to walk the Postman's Path around Shap. Details can be found at https://cutt.ly/RQFNvF0, but be aware it is a long and tough walk.*

† Sleddale Hall is the location used for Uncle Monty's cottage in the cult film Withnail and I.

ALWAYS SNOW AT CHRISTMAS

EVA Elliott has lived all her life in and around Whitehaven. She is now in her 90s and has happy memories of past Christmases and "winters when it always snowed".

Personal account, as told to the author, 2021.

I used to go to Crosthwaite School, which no longer exists, and there was always a nativity play. I played Mary and remember taking a china doll to use as the baby Jesus that I had probably received as a Christmas present the year before – though my cousin George later ended up breaking it!

My mother, Cissy, was very good at crafts and we would spend the days before Christmas making decorations for the tree – we didn't have baubles to buy in those days.

My dad, Joseph, used to love taking me shopping in the market in Whitehaven – it was much bigger than it is today – but I only realised when I was older that he was really watching me to see what I might want for a Christmas present.

I used to write a letter to Father Christmas and you had to throw the letter on the fire and hope that it was taken up the chimney. I never asked for much. I liked books and received a *Rainbow* annual every year. Jigsaws were a popular gift, and my brother John and I would receive packs of cards and dominoes; it was playing dominoes that helped teach my brother how to count. One of my favourite presents ever was a John Bull printing set. I also remember receiving a Toblerone chocolate – not in the triangular shape you see today, but in the shape of a bear. It was lovely, but I've never seen one since. We also received chocolate selection boxes.

My brother and I would wake up early – while it was still dark – and open the presents in the stockings at the end of our bed. These were mainly small gifts, but we always got an apple, orange or other piece of fruit. Then we would go downstairs and all the main presents were under the tree. I had an aunt who was a great knitter and there would be a jumper or cardigan. We were delighted, but I think today's children would be rather disappointed if they received a cardigan! I received a knitted Fairisle beret one Christmas and thought it was the bee's knees.

Mother worked as a cook at a restaurant on Lowther Street, so was very busy. In those days women had to give up work when they got married, but they were always asking her back. She even used to cook for Lord Lonsdale at the Castle in Whitehaven. This meant food was an important part of our Christmas.

Christmas dinner was chicken, followed by mince pies and a plum pudding. We even had a plum pudding during the war, though I don't know where mum got the dried fruit from. We always ate well.

We shared Christmas dinner with Granny and Granda, and an aunt and uncle. There were Christmas crackers that came in a box of 12. In the afternoon we would play with our presents while the adults chatted. There was no television, of course, but we had a wireless, as my father loved his sport.

Church was, and still is, an important part of my life. In my childhood I used to go to the Town Mission, but we didn't go on Christmas Day itself. The church had a nativity as well, and there was the singing of carols. There were also concerts at the Oddfellows Hall on Lowther Street.

On Boxing Day we would visit other relatives in town – a tradition that continued until my parents died: relatives would come to our house on Christmas Day and over the next few days we would go and visit them.

I remember winters being colder when I was younger – and there was always snow at Christmas! ❄

THE OLD FOLKS' CHRISTMAS DO

CHRISTMAS, as Scrooge discovered, is a time for charity, community and goodwill to all men. In the early 1900s the old folk of Keswick looked forward to an annual Christmas 'Do', with a heady mix of readings, recitations and song.

'A Rambler's Note-book at the English Lakes', Canon H. D. Rawnsley, 1902.

I DOUBT if there is any part of Great Britain where the tradition of holidays at Christmas time is so real and abiding as in the dales of Cumberland and Westmoreland. It is quite true that the old 'merry neets' have passed away; the farmers no longer take it in turn to call their neighbours and acquaintances together to a Christmas supper and 'three-card lant' and loo. Even so, whist parties remain the order of the day in many of the fell-side farms. I have talked with men who have played whist through the whole night, the whole of the next day, and part of the next night also, with such intervals for rest and refreshment as were necessary. In the air at Christmas time there is a sense – good both for man and beast – that there should be rest till Twelfth Night has come. There is a perceptible slackening of effort to do work, and a tacit recognition that, if orders for work are given, the person who gives them must not be surprised that the work remains over till the feeling for holiday is out of the blood.

Keswick and the neighbourhood are no exception in this matter, and I was not surprised to find on the day after Christmas Day that all the bodies who were able and strong on their feet had gathered together in the little Keswick market-place by nine o'clock in the morning to meet John Crozier's hounds and 'gang wid em for a la'al bit o' spoort on Skidder's breast'*.

The hounds came twinkling round the Royal Oak corner, and stood about the red-coated running huntsman, listening with apparent pleasure to the magnificent chorus of 'D'ye ken John Peel?' with which their coming had been welcomed. Scarce had the sound of 'Auld Lang Syne' died away when the whole market-place seemed to take to its heels, and the crowd moved up Main Street and over the Greta Bridge, away through Lime Pots by Vicarage Hill and down through the meadows – still grey and white with fadin' of snow – towards Millbeck and the Dodd.

Half-an-hour after they had passed I heard the sound of a horn and the cry of the hounds from afar, and I knew the game was afoot and that the Christmas hunt had begun in earnest. But my thoughts were not so much with the young men who were going to get a good 'breather' on Dodd, or the middle-aged folk who were going to dream over again the days of Christmas hunting years ago; I was thinking of the old folk – men and women of 60 years and upward – who were to be assembled today in the Oddfellows' Hall to partake of what is known as the 'Old Folks' Christmas Dinner and Tea', with whatever entertainment of reading, recitation, song and speech should make time pass pleasantly between three and seven o'clock.

I had an invitation to be present, and as I wished to see an old-fashioned Cumberland 'Do', I made my way thither towards three o'clock in the afternoon.

'Bus load after 'bus load came rumbling up, bringing out of the countryside the guests from distant hamlet and farm. Not less than 400 invitations had been sent out, and no less than 180 old folk had responded. The institution was unique in its way: 30 years ago it occurred to the writer of one of the best guidebooks that exists in the English Lake District, Jenkinson by name – an enthusiastic Yorkshireman who was domiciled at Keswick – that it would be a pleasant thing to have a social gathering to which all classes might be invited in Christmas week, and to which all who came should feel that they were there, not as it were by charity, but simply met together to chat with one another and enjoy themselves on equal terms as friends. Jenkinson's idea was warmly taken up by the leading townsmen, and from that day to this the annual Old Folks' Do has been looked forward to all through the year, and looked back upon with pleasantest memory.

On arriving at the entrance to the Hall, I found the local band making brave music. Passing up the steps by kitchens whose steamy fragrance filled the air, I was ushered into a large room decked with Christmas evergreen. Five tables reached from end to end, daintily decorated with ferns and flowers. The vicar of Crosthwaite, the county councillor of Keswick, the local lawyer, bank managers and leading hotel keepers were seated in the place of honour as carvers, and, after a whistle was sounded by the master of ceremonies, all rose to their feet, grace was said, and the chairman (begging no-one to hurry) impressed upon the company that the oldest and youngest were to take time today. Then soup was served.

At another whistle, soup was removed and the meats were borne into the room. Beef, turkey, mutton and goose were all there piping hot; potatoes, peas, pudding, turnips and other vegetables steamed on the tables. The chairman called for order and announced, as if it were a matter of most urgent importance, that giblet pies innumerable were downstairs, and anybody who wanted giblet pie had simply to say the word.

There was plenty to eat and drink. For those who cared for it, there was beer – but a very large proportion seemed to prefer lemonade, which was seen in syphons all down the table. There was not much talking; three o'clock was a late dinner hour for many of the old folks, and they were hungry. But as hunger passed away, the talk grew, and very pleasant it was to see the folk who had not met for a whole year cracking with one another, and to hear the little bits of family gossip, to ask how so-and-so has fared and what so-and-so is doing now.

Of course, there was an element of sadness in the room. The 180 people past 60 years meant 180 hearts that had seen much sorrow. Nevertheless, they appeared determined for the moment to forget the past and to think happily of the future.

After the meats came plum pudding. Again the chairman solemnly assured the company that for those who had few teeth in their heads or had eaten so many plum puddings that they had ceased to care for them, there was an abundance of rice pudding prepared, which was very much at their service. Mince pies seemed to be a kind of necessary second course to this plum pudding and rice. Then the whistle sounded again, and cheese and butter and biscuits were the order of the day. After about an hour, the tables were cleared and grace was said, and the bulk of the old folks left the hall for the carpenters to make their arrangements for the concert staging. They returned in half-an-hour and took their seats again at the tables for the entertainment, which was broken half way by an interval for tea and cake.

I saw the programme and knew that I was in for a long sitting, but it was so varied that it passed without fatigue. It was begun by the elementary scholars of one of the Keswick schools, under command of their master, singing four glees and reciting the ballad of 'The Revenge'†. Then a stalwart fox-hunter mounted the platform and gave with admirable voice and spirit 'We'll all go a-hunting today'. At the end of each verse, he shouted: "Now all together", and one felt the roof would be lifted as the 180 guests of 60 years and upwards joined in, with full accord, to assure the singer "that they would all go a-hunting to-day".

One or two songs followed, and the chairman gave his address. An excellent Cumberland dialect reading was given, and then tea was served. Then a fiddler mounted the platform, and the chairman solemnly begged the company to remove their cloos‡. I did not even know what a cloo was, but I soon found out the point of his remark. Hardly had the fiddler begun than the feet of all those aged people were heard keeping time to the fiddler's tune.

That love of dancing and sense of rhythm is native to Cumberland, and although days are past when elementary schools had to be closed because the dancing master had come into the neighbourhood, dancing is still a passion with the people, who seem better able to express themselves in that way than in any other. Suddenly the fiddler changed his tune to an old-fashioned eight-reel, and an aged woman rose from her seat and with the accustomed cry was seen to begin to dance as she had danced 70 years ago. It was an astonishing performance; I was told she was over 80, and in good truth, I believe if the chairman had not stopped the fiddler, she would have danced till she died. Great applause followed, and the old lady resumed her seat as if nothing remarkable had happened.

The proceedings ended with the National Anthem and a verse of 'Auld Lang Syne', which filled the room and echoed out into Keswick streets. Then, after many a hand-shaking and "Ye'll be here next year likely," "Ay, ay, I whoape sea," they passed back to the town and back in the omnibuses to the far-off farms and hamlets, and the Old Folks' 'Do' of 1901 was past and over. ❄

**Hunting on foot has a long association with the northern fells. Caldbeck's most famous son – and Master of Foxhounds – was John Peel.*

† 'The Revenge' was a popular poem and ballad written by Alfred Lord Tennyson in 1878, telling the tale of a British warship sunk by a Spanish Armada in 1591.

‡ Cloos – Clothes, i.e. take their coats off ready to dance.

CHRISTMAS IN THE WORKHOUSE

WORKHOUSES opened in the 18th century as a way of helping the poor, but public perception of them as 'pauper's palaces' forced authorities to make them more austere. By the 19th century they were places to be avoided, with the very poor and their children toiling to earn their keep. Only at Christmas did the public show a semblance of charity to those in poverty – though gifting alcohol was often a step too far...

'Carlisle Journal', 27 December, 1850.

CARLISLE

THE inmates of St Mary's Workhouse in Carlisle were plentifully regaled with the good old English fare of roast beef and plum pudding. The dining room was decorated with evergreens and fruit, and at the extremity of the table was a splendid iced plum cake, benevolently presented to the inmates by Mr John Ritson. Ample justice having been done to the more substantial repast, each individual was presented with a pint of ale and supply of tobacco, over the discussion of which the health of the Queen, and of the dean and his lady, the guardians and governor &c was given and responded to.

In the afternoon, through the kindness of the matron, the inmates were supplied with tea and cakes. The day was most cheerfully spent, and all seemed delighted with the kind hospitality so seasonably bestowed upon them.

'The Westmorland Gazette', 31 December, 1864.

CARLISLE

AT the Board of Guardians, on Thursday, extra provisions was made for the Christmas dinner of the inmates of the workhouse, and indulgences were to be allowed consistent with the good order of the House. A guardian suggested that such of the old people as wished it should have beer, but it was thought by another that, as some of them owed their tenancy in that place to the influence of beer, it would be better to keep it out of the House altogether. This course was decided upon, but an extra pipe of tobacco was allowed.

'The Cumberland Pacquet', 28 December, 1893.

WHITEHAVEN

CHRISTMAS was observed at the Whitehaven Union Workhouse in the customary festive style. A capital dinner of roast beef and plum pudding was provided for all the inmates, who also received various little delicacies and seasonable gifts from a number of kind-hearted friends. The spacious dining hall, in which the repast was served about half-past 12 o'clock on Christmas Day, was most elaborately decorated with holly, laurel leaves, ivy and other evergreens, which covered the walls, arches, rafters and window sills in the form of festoons and other devices. Four fir trees were displayed in conspicuous positions, and other branches were arranged with toys and other articles for the children. On a white ground, fringed with laurel leaves, was the seasonable greeting 'A merry Christmas and a happy New

Year'. Another motto on the wall was 'God save the Queen'. The decorations, which were much admired, reflected great credit on the artistic abilities of Mr and Mrs Dixon, the master and matron, under whose direction they were carried out.

The inmates who partook of the Christmas fare numbered about 340. The number of children now in the Workhouse is above the average. About 68 stones of beef had been cut up for the dinner from the carcase of a blue-grey bullock which had been fed by Mr R. Jefferson, of Rothersyke, and which was purchased at the Whitehaven fat stock show by Mr Oliver Hodgson, the butcher who has the contract for supplying the workhouse with meat. Gifts donated to the Workhouse included toys, sweets, picture books, oranges, toffee, tobacco, tea and nuts.

'The Westmorland Gazette', 1 January, 1898.

MILNTHORPE

THE fine weather made the few days before Christmas very enjoyable for both visitors and inhabitants, and the frozen waters at Haverbrack and other places were well patronised. On Christmas Eve the usual charities were disbursed, the two bands of music discoursed until a late hour, and the waits (minstrels) went their rounds. Christmas Day at church was heralded by early celebration, followed by the morning service. The singing was specially bright, the usual hymns and an anthem being given. The sacred edifice was very tastefully decorated by a number of ladies.

At the workhouse, the inmates appeared to enjoy immensely the roast beef and plum pudding, and Mr and Mrs Huck had a busy time satisfying the demands of the old and young folks. For the first time, fruitcake was served for tea. Hearty cheers were given for the guardians and others for their kindness. The dining room, under the hands of inmates and officers, was very prettily ornamented with evergreens and floral designs.

Amongst the presents received by the inmates was six pence each to all the aged and infirm from the chairman of the Guardians, 12 couples of rabbits and a large basket of apples from Sir Henry Bromley, 100 mince pies from Mrs Cary, 50 shawls from the ladies' committee, and an unknown friend sent some tobacco and snuff.

'Carlisle Gazette', 15 December, 1925.

CARLISLE

By a large majority, Carlisle Guardians yesterdays decided that the inmates of the Workhouse should not receive beer with their Christmas dinner. Mr Wright, in proposing that beer be given, said that, in view of the forthcoming abolition of the Guardians, he would not like it to go down to posterity that they refused the inmates a Christmas glass of beer. Miss Musgrave said the inmates should have a little extra at Christmastide. Miss Watson said if they did not allow beer, the temperance people would be applying force to the inmates inside the institution which they could not impose outside. Mr Briggs said the inmates would rather have a cup of tea than all the beer that was brewed. The opponents of the proposal to allow beer included members of the local temperance body. ❄

PEEL'S YULETIDE PARTY

AUTHOR Hugh Walpole (1884–1941) was born in New Zealand, but made the Lakes his home, living for many years on the shores of Derwent Water. He was a great advocate of Cumberland, and in his book 'Rogue Herries' – part of the once best-selling Herries Chronicles saga – he included the following detailed sketch of a rural statesman's Christmas.

'Rogue Herries', Hugh Walpole, 1930.

THAT was the happiest evening they had yet had in Borrowdale. The hall was bright, the fire leaping, the candles burning, the floor shining. Wilson had hung three old flags that had been buried in the oak chest, one of crimson with a white cross, one of faded purple and one of green. Whose flags? From what wars? No-one knew. The holly was thick with red berries that year and hung from the rafters. They could hear the bells ringing from the chapel above the splash and crackle of the fire.

Next night, Christmas night, they were invited to Statesman Peel's*. It was not as it was in most parts of England where, at Christmas time, the Squire was the king of the castle and his subjects were graciously bidden to enjoy his hospitality with a proper sense of his grand benignancy and their inferior peasantry. In Borrowdale every Statesman was master of his own house and owed allegiance to no-one. Every Statesman's house was open on Christmas night to all the world, rich and poor. There were the guests, indeed, who had their special places there, but the doors were wide open to the stars and the line of friendly hills and the hard-frosted road.

Peel's kitchen this night was a place of splendour. Its warmth and colour, its happiness and hospitality, stretched to the farthest heavens. Glaramara and the Gavel looked in at the windows, the Derwent rolled its waters past the door, and every star scattered its light over the roof-tree.

There is no house like Peel's house anywhere in England any more, but, as it stood then, in its life and strength and happiness, it was thus. It was a strong place, secured with strong doors and gates, its small windows crossed with bars of iron. It held three rooms on the ground floor and two on the second storey. The front door was covered with a low porch, the entrance from which was called the 'thresh-wood' or threshold, and on this thresh-wood crossed straws, horse-shoes and so on, were laid to hinder the entrance of witches. From this there was a broad passage through the house called the 'hallan'; sacks of corn were deposited here before market day, pigs were hung after killing, and there was a shelf over the door where sickles hung and carpentry tools were laid.

In Peel's house the hallan opened straight into the 'downhouse'. This was the great common room of the family, and the place of tonight's Christmas feast. Here, in the course of the year, everything occurred: baking, brewing, washing, meals, quarrelling, courting, tale-telling. This downhouse had no second storey, but was open to the rafters. In later days a second storey was often built over the downhouse. The sides of this room were smeared with clay and cow-dung. Joints of meat hung dry for winter use. From the smoky dome of the huge fireplace dropped a black sooty lee called the 'hallan drop'. Under this the women knitted or spun wool or flax, the men sometimes carding the wool, the children learning their lessons, the old men telling their tales. At the opposite end of the passage was the mill-door, and beyond this was another passage known as the 'heck', and this heck was terminated by a huge octagonal post. Into this post sometimes a hole was bored and in it a piece of cow-hair secured by a wooden peg for the purpose of cleaning combs.

The chimney wing was spacious. Indeed, this was a really vast chamber, for it was the 'house' or dwelling-room and 'downhouse' or kitchen thrown into one. Part of it, therefore, stood for kitchen with the great chimney and hearth; here, on the heap of wood ashes, was the 'handreth', an iron tripod on which was placed the 'girdle' for baking oat-bread.

Before the fire stood a spit. The two standards, which were three feet high with seven hooks, were hinged, so that they could be folded and put away when not in use. The spit, a slender rod, was six feet in length, and on the rod were two pairs of prongs to hold the meat, and beneath it a dripping-pan. There was a handmill or 'quern', a malt mill, a spindle and a 'whorl' – a spinning wheel. In the chimney wing were hung hams and sides of bacon and beef, and near the fire-window was an ingle-seat, comfortable most of the year save when the rain or snow poured down on to the hearth, as the chimney was quite unprotected and you could look up it and see the sky above you. Such was the kitchen end of the room. The floor to-night was cleared for dancing, but at the opposite end trestle-tables were ranged for feasting. Here was also a large oak cupboard with handsomely carved doors. This held the bread, made of oatmeal and water. On the mantel and cupboard there were rush-light holders and brass candlesticks. In other parts of the room were big standard holders for rush-lights.

Francis Herries, arriving with his children, David, Mary and Deborah, found that already everything was in a whirl. Peel himself greeted them magnificently, standing his six foot four, splendid in his dark coat of native fleece and buckskin breeches, and Mrs.

Peel, stout, very red of face, in russet, all the little Peels (and there were very many) gathered together behind her.

Many were already dancing. It was a scene of brilliant colour with the blazing fire, the red berries of the holly glowing in every corner, old Johnny Shoestring in bright blue breeches and with silver buckles to his shoes perched on a high stool fiddling for his life, the brass gleaming, faces shining, the stamp of the shoes, the screaming of the fiddle, the clap-clap of the hands as the turns were made in the dance, and, beyond the heat and light, the dark form of the valley lying in breathless stillness, its face stroked by the fall of lingering reluctant snow.

After the first greeting, the Herries family stood quietly by the wall. Fragments of talk – slow cautious words like the repetition of some magic recipe – circled the light.

"Hoo ayre ye to-day? Hey ye hard ony news?"...

"Ye say reet, nowt se sartain. Gud day. Ayre ye all weel at heam?"

"Aye, they said she was worth brass..."

"Whya, he's nobbut read about it; what can he knaw? I sud think if he minds his awn job it'll be as weel."

The door would open and the snow blow through in little impatient gusts and all the valley would pour in with it. The room was crowded now against the wall and in the corners. The ale was passing round, and voices were loud and laughter ferocious. But everyone behaved in seemly fashion; a dignity that seemed to radiate from the grand figure and quiet hospitality of the host himself pervaded the place. Only – as Francis Herries could feel; he could sniff it in the air – there was a kind of madness behind the dignity, something that belonged to the witches and old crippled warlocks, to the naked shapes playing under the stars above Seatoller, to the broomsticks flying dimly like thin clouds towards the moon.

Suddenly there was a cry: "They coom. They're here." It was the 'play-jigg'. This was the drama in verse played by the actors who, tonight, were passing from Statesman's house to Statesman's house. Johnny Shoestring ceased his playing, the dancers vanished, the centre of the room was clear. Packed against the walls now were bodies and faces, legs and backs. There was whispering and tittering, but quite clearly in the immediate silence could be heard the hiss of snow hovering down through the open chimney onto the fire.

They came forward. Francis was amused as he saw that the master of these ceremonies was his old friend the pedlar, David's Devil. Very roguish he was tonight in a cocked purple hat and purple tights showing his thin, spidery limbs, his face with its crooked ironic smile, and his black shining eyes.

He introduced his little company: Old Giles, a bent old man with a long chin; Pinch, a clown – a stout and jolly fellow; a husband and a wife; and young Go-to-Bed who, at once in a high, shrill treble, introduced himself:

> My father is old and decrepit,
> My mother deceased of late,
> And I am a youth that's respected,
> Possessed of a good estate.

The old couple did a little dance of joy at this, and then Pinch the clown came forward and asked young Go-to-Bed if he wanted to increase his fortune. Of course young Go-to-Bed was eager, so Pinch introduced him to Old Giles, who said he would show him how to make money out of nothing. This young Go-to-Bed was delighted to know, so Old Giles told him that he must have his arse kicked a dozen times by friend Pinch, and then he must put his head in a bucket of water and then must sit up a night alone in a churchyard: all these things young Go-to-Bed performed to the infinite delight of the audience, especially in the churchyard when Pinch, dressed as a painful ghost, emptied a sack of flour over young Go-to-Bed and set the dogs on him.

The 'jigg' ended in a grand dance, and in this the audience soon joined. Go-to-Bed, his face white with flour, led off with Mrs. Peel, and Peel took the Old Lady, and soon all the room was turning to Johnny Shoestring's music. ❄

** A statesman farmer was one who owned his farm and land – as opposed to a tenant farmer, more common in other parts of the north country.*

CHRISTMAS WITH THE WORDSWORTHS

"ALL look forward to your arrival as to the holly branch, without which no Christmas will be genuine. I always sing the same song – No Crabb, no Christmas." So wrote William Wordsworth to his friend Henry Crabb Robinson, a visitor each Christmas in Grasmere. Robinson's diaries give a glimpse into his visits to William Wordsworth, wife Mary and the poet's sister, Dorothy.

'The Diaries of Henry Crabb Robinson', Ed. Morley J. Edith, 1938.

CHRISTMAS Day, 1835: I was set down at a small house at the foot of Rydal Hill, kept by a Mrs Atkins. Here I found a fire in the sitting-room intended for me. Mrs Wordsworth had left tea and sugar for me, and I saw an omen of comfort in this lodging in the agreeable countenance of my landlady. Without waiting to dress, I ran up to the Wordsworths, from whom I had a very kind reception... Mrs [Mary] Wordsworth was what I have ever known her: perfect of her kind. I did not know her when [she] was the 'phantom of delight', but ever since I have known her she has been:

> A perfect woman, nobly planned
> To warm, to comfort, and command.

Because she is so admirable a person, there is little to say of her in detail.

We dined as they do usually here – very early. One is the dinner hour, and the rest of the day was spent within, except that we took a walk after dinner; that is, Wordsworth and myself (beyond Dr. Arnold's house with the Doctor himself to his house), and I came home at nine. Read till past 12, when I retired, having at night begun Southey's 'Life of Cowper'.

26 December: I read in bed a couple of hours, for I awoke early. I sat within – not till dinner-time as it happened – for about 12 [o'clock] Mrs. Wordsworth passing in a gig proposed my taking Wordsworth out. I called on him and we had a fine dry walk up Grasmere lake, crossed it, and returned on the west side. I stayed with the Wordsworths, as I generally shall do, the rest of the day, and in the dark hour I walked with Wordsworth by Grasmere lake, also down to Ambleside – the excuse, to ask for a paper. We returned to our tea at six, and at nine I came home, having ordered a fire in my bedroom at which I sat till 12, when I read in bed till one.

Such will probably be my life for the next few weeks. I am most comfortably situated. My kind and agreeable landlady makes me excellent toast and I have my own tea – a ham has been supplied by Mrs. Wordsworth. In the evening I take a morsel of bread and ham to keep off the foul fiend. [I stay in] a cottage-like apartment, very comfortable, a similar bedroom behind; for this I am to pay (Mrs. Wordsworth says) ten shillings a week, and three and sixpence for fire. I dare say I shall be most honestly charged for the few things I consume.

27 December: I read early Southey's 'Cowper' till church time. I went to church. [There was] but a small congregation in this neat ornament to the village (a chapel-of-ease). Dr. Arnold officiated;

he has the face and voice and manner of a man of talents, but his sermon was altogether cold – as bad as the morning itself: I sat shivering without my great coat.

We dined at one. After dinner I walked with Wordsworth by Grasmere and to Ambleside, though it rained a little; at nine I came home. Today full of conversation; it gave me great pleasure to perceive that both Mrs and Dora Wordsworth are evidently gratified by my being here. They say I have already done Wordsworth a great service by taking him out of himself; both they and he were in better spirits than I could have expected, and Dora* – a very sweet girl – is evidently in improving health; Wordsworth is somewhat less intolerant than he used to be and we have had very little sparring yet on politics. At night I finished Southey's first volume of Cowper's 'Life' – a very uncomfortable book – no fault of the writer's. He could not have satisfied his employers if he had not given a full account of Cowper's diseased religion. The only amusing parts are the digressive accounts of Churchill and Lloyd.

28 December: A day of uninterrupted quiet enjoyment. I looked over an important document (Wordsworth's Will), which required attention and thought, and I continued Lamb's letters till one. After dinner I chatted with Wordsworth and between three and four we set out, notwithstanding the bad weather, for it had rained all morning and threatened to rain again.

We strolled onto the shore of Windermere. The angry clouds left Langdale Pikes a grand object – more grand, perhaps, surrounded by black stormy clouds than illumined by the sun – and we made several calls. ❄

* *Dora was one of William and Mary's daughters.*

CHRISTMAS ON THE FARM

Thomas Park Benson was born in 1916 near Ulverston. His biography, *As I Return To Yesteryear*, includes memories of Christmas on the family farm.

'As I Return To Yesteryear', Thomas Park Benson, 1982.

THE great day arrived, bringing its visit from Father Christmas, and the toys which a few weeks before had been on Waston's toy stall in the old market house at Ulverston: a Mama Doll for Joan*, a Meccano set for myself, and – for the boy who was destined to become the farmer of the family, brother Dick – a model farmyard and lead-painted animals. A tin of Sharpe's toffee and a stocking stuffed with various odds-and-ends completed the booty.

The farm men and girls exchanged small presents: a packet of cigars, razor blades, Woodbines – maybe a mouth organ for the nipper lad. The girls received Yardley's lavender water, Pear's toilet soap and a bar of Cadbury's milk chocolate. Mother gave each of them an orange and an apple, together with a small bag of mixed nuts. The farm animals were not ignored. Dogs got an extra feed of oatmeal porridge or potatoes, the cows an unthreshed sheaf of oats, and the work horses a feed of boiled oats and sweet molasses.

The large goose was usually a bird that had been difficult to pluck, and did not show itself off too well, but the meat was just as tender and no less delicious. Each of us in his or her own mind thanked the Lord for his bounty and goodness as we ate this Christmas dinner.

The Christmas pudding was boiled in a large pan, and as it was unfolded from its cloth surroundings and served, together with real rum sauce, the search began for small silver three-penny bits that had been placed in it by my father. "I've got one, I've got one!", cried the nipper as he took the wrapped silver bit from his mouth – his joy complete.

Mince pies and boiling hot tea finished off a satisfying repast.

It was a holy day – a day of rest – and the only work done was the tending of animals and milking. Later on, a special tea of jellies, trifle and beautiful Christmas cake, covered in icing, was enjoyed.

At night, after completing the milking, the men and girls who lived close to their homes changed into their Sunday clothes, got out their bikes and took off to spend a few hours at home in the bosom of their families.

Maybe some neighbour would drop in for a few hands of cards with my parents. However, by then, we were tired out after a hectic, exciting day and soon we were head for the land of nod. ❄

* *Mama Dolls were patented in 1918 by Georgene Averill. When tilted, a mechanical voice box in the doll would cause it to cry 'Mama'.*

VISIT FROM THE SKIES

IN 1926, daredevil pilots of those new-fangled flying machines – aeroplanes – were attempting ever-more daring feats. Days before Christmas, one landed on the summit of Helvellyn. Youngsters watching must have thought Father Christmas had arrived early and traded in poor Rudolph for more modern transportation...

'Hull Daily Mail', 23 December, 1926.

JOHN Leeming, the well-known Lancashire airman, yesterday afternoon succeeded in landing his aeroplane on the summit of Helvellyn, 3,100 feet above sea level. This was his third attempt, the object being to prove that modern aircraft has so improved as to permit safe landing in almost inaccessible places.

A week ago, when he made his first attempt, Mr Leeming was accompanied in another machine by Mr Bert Hinkler, the famous pilot who flew in the Schneider Cup race. They were defeated by fog, which entirely obscured the upper reaches of the mountain.

On Tuesday, a second attempt was made in strong wind, but the gale which they encountered in the mountain ranges was so fierce that Mr Leeming and Hinkler, who on this occasion were flying together in an Avro Gosport machine, were driven back and landed at Lancaster, where engine trouble developed and where they stayed overnight. Yesterday morning, conditions were more favourable, and the airmen started on their third attempt at mid-day. The landing was safely accomplished at 1.35 p.m.

By his fine success in landing on Helvellyn – ranking as one of the highest peaks in England, with its summit standing 3,118 feet – Mr Bert Hinkler and his companion, J. Leeming, have cut another niche in the history of flying. Their success, moreover, is further proof of the indomitable spirit possessing Britishers, for two well-planned efforts had failed within a week, despite which these intrepid souls set out without any preparations for landing or welcome, and achieved their object. It is this lack of preparation which makes the feat stand out, for there was no-one below to indicate a favourable landing spot, or smoke trails to show the way of the wind, yet ground was safely reached on a rough portion of Mother Earth, much higher than the site prepared a week ago, and within ten yards of the summit.

Happily for the airmen, and for the public generally, there can be no doubt that the task was achieved, for an unexpected host was met in Professor E. R. Dodds – a distinguished scholar of Birmingham University who includes mountaineering among his hobbies – who by a fortuitous chance was exploring the mysteries of Helvellyn when the airmen dropped from the sky. Moreover, photographs are available showing the gauntness of the scene. These, in company with certificate from Professor Dodds, preclude any possibility of the claim being a spoof on the public.

The most difficult part of the attempt docs not appear to have been the landing, but the mighty air pockets encountered. Mr Leeming declared they were the worst he had ever known, for in one of them they experienced a drop of 500 feet. The fall was so swift that somewhere in the upper air was left a letter they had intended to post in Thirlmere, and another loss was that of a cushion in this awful slip. Happily, both occupants of the 'plane had made use of their safety belts, else another story might have had to be written about the mastering of this peak of Keswick and Ambleside. Compared with this nerve-racking experience, the actual landing appears to have been a comparatively simple affair, for after circling three times in a descending spiral, the machine came to safety some 23 yards from the edge of a precipice and on such rising ground that the engine had to be kept running on almost full throttle until one of the occupants jumped out and banked up the wheels with stones to prevent a run down the mountain side.

The effort was a daring one, to which there might have been an unfortunate climax, but the success should go far towards alleviating fears in the minds of pilots forced to descend, for the atmospherical conditions and ground were as bad as any likely to be encountered in the ordinary way flying along the ever-expanding commercial routes.

It was a fine exhibition ability on the part of men and machine, but though lovers of quiet places will applaud the feat its true merit, they will hope that it is not to become common that airmen are to intrude into the fastness of our country. Valuable, and indeed essential as they are, there are some landscapes wherein the hum of an aeroplane sounds a discordant note.

It cannot be said that by their flight Messrs Hinkler and Leeming intended to spoil some picnic party, but there is danger that with the continued growth of aviation, the pleasant retreats and side-lanes of our country will become as fearsome to lovers of tranquillity as are the main roads to the modern pedestrian, who has to concentrate far more on the dangers of motorists than the joy of getting his best leg forward. ❄

LATE NIGHT MERRY-MAKING

WHAT epitomises Christmas for you? Publisher William Hone produced a number of magazines in the 19th century that featured articles from regional contributors. For this Cumberland correspondent nearly 200 years ago, Christmas meant dining with family and friends, playing cards, drinking punch, eating mince pies and assorted other 'merry-making'.

'Hone's Year Book of 1827', William Hone.

NOWHERE does the Christmas season produce more heart-inspiring mirth than among the inhabitants of Cumberland. The farmer may be seen with his hands enveloped in huge mittens, thrust half-way into his breeches' pockets, and his fustian jacket buttoned well up under his chin, jogging merrily along to his daily labour, singing or whistling as he goes, whilst his jolly red face – scarcely perceivable on account of the dense fog – appears like the sun dimly seen through mist.

The tarns may be seen covered with boys, some with wisps of straw brushing off the snow, others sliding in wooden clogs, which are more convenient for this purpose than shoes. They exhort each other to 'keep the pot boiling'* 'till perhaps one of them falls, and the next, on account of the velocity, and not being able to stop, stumbles over him, and so on, until most of them lie rolling in a heap together, to the great joy of their comrades, who cry out: "my pot boils over," and with all their might endeavour to prevent them from getting up.

Sliding by moonlight is very common here, because the men – not having been able to leave work in the day time – think it fine opportunity to enjoy their favourite amusement, 'shurelin'†.

In the farmhouse, we may find the good dame and her rosy-cheeked daughters busied in preparing mince pies, raised pies⁑, tarts and other good things, which indicate that something particular is about to take place. In short, with Christmas Eve commences a regular series of 'festivities and merry-makings'.

Night after night, if you want the farmer or his family, you must look for them anywhere but at home, and in the different houses that you pass at one, two or three in the morning – should you happen to be out so late – you will find candles and fires still unextinguished. At Christmas, every farmer gives two 'feasts', one called 't' auld foaks' neet', which is for those who are married, and the other 't' young foaks' neet', for those who are single.

Suppose you and I, sir, take the liberty of attending one of these feasts unasked (which, by the by, is considered no liberty at all in Cumberland), and see what gome on...

Upon entering the room, we behold several card parties, some at whist, others at loo (there called 'lant') or any other game that may suit their fancy.

You will be surprised looking ever the company to find that there is no distinction of persons. Masters and servants, rich and poor, humble and lofty; all mingle together without restraint – all cares are forgotten – and each one seems to glory in his own enjoyment and in that of his fellow creatures. It is pleasant to find ourselves in such society – especially as it is rarely in one's life that such opportunities offer.

Cast your eyes towards the sideboard and there see that large bowl of punch, which the good wife is inviting her guests to partake of, with apples, oranges, biscuits, and other agreeable eatables in plenty. The hospitable master welcomes with a smiling countenance and requests us to take seats and join one of the tables.

In due time someone enters to tell the company that supper is waiting in the next room. Thither we adjourn, and find the raised and mince pies, all sorts of tarts, and all cold – except the welcomes and entreaties – with cream, ale. &c., in abundance. In the midst of all is a large goose pie, which seems to say: "Come an' cut again."

After supper, the party returns to the card room, sits there for two or three hours longer, and afterwards makes the best of their way home, to take good long nap and prepare for the same scene the next night.

At these feasts intoxication is entirely out of the question – it never happens. Such are the innocent amusements of these people, and, hoping that you may sometime have an opportunity of visiting this part of the country, and of being present in reality at the scenes I have described,

– I remain, sir, yours respectfully, A. R.

* *Keep the pot boiling – To sustain some action; to keep up an activity for a long time.*
† *Shurelin – Curling, a game played on ice.*
‡ *Raised pies – Crusty pies. The traditional method of baking them involved moulding the pie around a wooden dolly (stick) by hand.*

THE CHRISTMAS TRUCE

CUMBRIAN soldiers were among those who took part in the remarkable Christmas Truce of 1914 on the Western front. On Christmas Day – a cold, misty morning – opposing soldiers lay down their arms, crossed no-man's-land and shook hands with the 'enemy'. Many wrote home about their experiences of singing carols together and sharing food, drink and gifts. Below are extracts from their astonishing letters.

Letter from a Maryport Private, 15 January, 1915.

YOU need not have pitied us on Christmas Day; I have seldom spent a more entertaining one, despite the curious conditions. We were in the trenches and the Germans began to make merry on Christmas Eve shouting at us to come out and meet them. They sang songs (very well), our men answered by singing 'Who were you with last night?' and of course, 'Tipperary' (very badly). The private soldiers of one army and the private soldiers of the other arranged a 48 hours armistice. It was all most irregular. The enemy sang all night and during my watch they played 'Home Sweet Home' and 'God Save the King'. It was rather wonderful: the night was clear, cold and frosty, and across to our lines at this unusually miserable hour of night came the sound of such tunes very well played, especially by a man with a cornet who is probably well known.

Christmas Day was very misty, and out came these Germans to wish us "a happy day"; we went out and told them we were at war with them and that really they must play the game and pretend to fight; they went back, but again attempted to come towards us, so we fired over their heads; they fired a shot back to show they understood and the rest of the day passed quietly in this part of the line – though in others a deal of fraternising went on. So there you are; all this talk of hate, all this firing at each other that has raged since the beginning of the war, quelled and stayed by the magic of Christmas. Indeed one German said: "But you are of the same religion as us and today is the day of peace!" It is really a great triumph for the church, and a great hope for future peace when two great nations hating each other as foes have seldom hated, should on Christmas Day and for all that the word implies, lay down their arms, exchange smokes and wish each other happiness.

Thank you for your ripping parcel. We had a grand time over it. To crown all, one of the fellows sharing my hut had a parcel on the same day and we combined and invited four more pals, one of whom had a box of Tom Smith Christmas crackers sent out, which we cracked, and it added to the fun immensely. Christmas in the trenches? What a time! "Peace on earth, goodwill toward men." Who can realise it? It will astound everyone who hears about it, which everyone will do in good time. Of course, I am speaking about the part of the firing line we are situated in.

On Christmas Eve at four p.m. we had orders that unless the 'enemy' advanced we were not to fire, and the same applied to Christmas Day. Whether the Germans had the same order, I don't know, but no shot was fired on either side. On Christmas Day, after service in the trenches, we went half way, shook hands and had a fine crack with them. Quite a number of them speak English. I got one's autograph and he got mine, and I exchanged a button with another, and exchanged cigs and got cigars galore. Altogether we spent a very pleasant two hours with them, and found them a nice lot of fellows. There is heaps more I should like to tell, but I know it would never get passed, so it will have to wait.

Letter from an officer in the Border Regiment,
'Carlisle Journal', 8 January, 1915.

LIFE is very peaceful here at present, as we have had a mutual truce with the Germans in front of us since Christmas morning. Our trenches are only about 100 yards away from the enemy's, and every day since Christmas we've been talking to them in the ground between. In normal times it's certain death to show your head above the parapet for more than four seconds, but now both sides are walking about openly. On Christmas morning the Germans gave us a burst of machine gun and rifle fire for about ten minutes and then shouted across "A Merry Christmas". Then one of the Germans got up and we picked him off. Then one of the Gordon Highlanders (on our left) got up and he was picked off. Then about 20 of ours and the same number of the Germans got up together, and we arranged a truce for Christmas Day.

This armistice has continued so far, and we have no desire to start scrapping again. Firing does no good, for both the Germans and ourselves are very strongly entrenched, and artillery is the only thing that can shift either of us. When firing is going on, ration and water parties have to use communication trenches to reach the firing line. When no firing is taking place, these fatigues are able to walk across country to the firing line which saves a great deal of time.

The trenches are not too bad if only the rain were a little less attentive. This district is wetter than the Lakes, and as the soil is very clayey, the mud is more than usually adhesive. ❄

GOODWILL TO ALL

BY the end of the 19th century, the traditions of Victorian yuletides were becoming ghosts of Christmas past. Author Thomas Gibson was pleased to note that folk from the north country were retaining the old traditions longer than most...

'Legends and Historical Notes on Places of North Westmoreland', Thomas Gibson, 1887.

AT no place does Christmas produce more heart-inspiring mirth than amongst the natives of Cumberland and Westmoreland. In the long winter evenings, card parties are invited, bowls of punch are not uncommon, while roast goose and plum puddings form the Christmas Day repast in many a farmhouse and substantial household.

The lads and lasses play off charades; amateur theatricals, glees, concerts and so forth are got up frequently at village parties; Christmas trees are procured for the children; and prizes are given for excellence in singing and drawing and other accomplishments.

Such are some of the amusements which Christmas annually produces. It unites the different members of the family under the paternal roof and cements the goodwill of each other towards their neighbours. There is often sadness felt from the absence of some near and dear one – perhaps gone away forever – but we cannot always live in the past. Our future should be brightened by such gatherings and our minds mellowed and hallowed by bereavement as we think of the yearly festivity, and celebrate the anniversary of that birth which gave 'glory to God and peace on earth toward men'. ❄

ON THE GRAMOPHONE

THE *Penrith Observer*'s music critic – 'The Pennine Warbler' – selects his 1930s top-of-the-Christmas-pops.

'The Penrith Observer', 16 December, 1930.

THERE is one subject which it is fitting and proper to discuss in these notes, and that is the contribution of the gramophone to the pleasures of Christmas. The gramophone companies, like our friend the postman, have not forgotten Christmas. The HMV products, in particular, are full of ingenious ideas. One of their brightest is a record called 'Musical Chairs'. It enables a party to play this indispensable Christmas game to the accompaniment of the New Mayfair Orchestra. There is also 'The Smoking Concert'*. Which of us does not remember the old-time smoking concert?! The smoking was always magnificent! Here it all is – almost to the smoke. ☞

But what about the young ones? Well here they are – with 'Uncle George's Party' in 'Nursery Rhymes'. Then for a new version of the guessing game... Not 'animal, vegetable or mineral' this time... All take pencil and paper and write down the names of the tunes played by the London Palladium Orchestra in 'Lightning Switch' with no cheating – remember – and no giving of tips to your fair neighbour, however pretty she may be!

For those who want some beautiful Christmas music, there is a record by the Philharmonic Choir from 'The Messiah' and another of the Westminster Abbey Choir in 'Hail, Holy Child' &C.

Two more records should be mentioned in this Christmas collection. The Covent Garden Orchestra play old carol tunes in 'A Noel Fantasy' and HMV have issued a new Harry Lauder in two songs – 'Somebody's Waiting For Me' and 'O'er The Hills To Ardentenny'. ❄

** Smoking concerts were musical performances popular in the Victorian era, during which men would smoke and speak politics while listening to live music.*

PART 2

YULETIDE HAUNTINGS

A GHOST CAUGHT ON CHRISTMAS EVE

THE Christmas ghost story is as much part of the season as mince pies and mulled wine. Here the *Whitehaven News* of 1899 relates the truth behind a famous Cumbrian legend...

'Whitehaven News', 21 December, 1899.

FIFTY years ago possibly there were no districts outside Scotland more thoroughly steeped in superstition and belief in the supernatural than southwest Cumberland and North Lonsdale, which adjoin each other. Every old hall, bridge and hollow in the highway had its ghosts, and few people cared to pass these places at night. Two halls in the vicinity of Ulverston were especially noted as bogey spots*; Plumpton Hall and Old Hall, formerly residential mansions, now occupied as farms.

It must not be forgotten that at the time of which we write the districts above alluded to were shut virtually out from the world; they had no railway communication, and few persons essayed a journey to London without first making their wills, for in addition to the other difficulties and dangers, there was first the long coach drive over the sands of Morecambe Bay†, in whose treacherous quicksands so many travellers have lost their lives.

The Plumpton Hall Dobby takes the unusual form of a brass hall lantern, harmless enough if left alone, but very unpleasant to those adventurous enough to touch it. It is stated that it has been taken long distances away from the hall, and has been sunk in the tide, but it has always been found back in its place when the household came down next morning.

The Old Hall Dobby was a much more active spirit. The house is situated under the shelter of a large wood, and doings of the ghost became noised abroad throughout the district, so that many persons visited the place, and some sought permission to sleep in the haunted chamber – some in the spirit of adventure, others actuated by a spirit of research into the mysteries of the supernatural. But one night was sufficient for the boldest, and the tales they told were of harrowing description – the groaning, the clanking of chains, the shrieks combined to make a perfect pandemonium of horrible sounds. They had fired pistols at the ghost, but it went on its way unharmed, although the bullets must have passed through it, and the strangest thing of all was that next morning there were neither bullets to be found, nor yet bullet marks on the walls. They could not understand how the farmer and his family dared live in the house; certainly in consequence of the ghosts, he held the farm as a nominal rent, but on no pecuniary consideration would they spend another night there... And so matters went on for years, and no-one questioned but that a ghost had its dwelling place at Old Hall.

At the close of the year 18--, it happened that Tom Jackson, who lived as a farm servant at the adjoining farm of Bartree Stile, situated at the top of Old Hall Wood, and a fellow female servant at the same farm (the two being sweethearts), were returning home from a Christmas Eve party.

A footpath runs through the top of the wood its full length and as the two were proceeding along this in the witching hours of the night, they were startled by a series of heart-rending groans and the clanking of chains. "The ghost, Tom! The ghost," shivered Mary, sinking down on her knees.

Barely had she uttered the exclamation when a fearful figure flitted past them. It was of more than man's stature, clothed in white, and on its head was a grinning fleshless human skull enveloped in light. Chains clanked horribly as it moved. Now, on the farm Tom was what they called a 'thinking devil' – that is, he had the habit of investigating for himself anything that came in his way.

As the ghost vanished out of sight, he took out his knife and cut down a supple ash plant: "Come, Mary, me lass, we've got to catch that ghost." Mary demured; it was flying in the face of Providence. "Well," said Tom, "thou ayder stops here or gangs wi'me. I's gain t'hey it hout wi' that ghost. What thou isent freetent when I's wi' thee?" Thus Mary followed down the wood, and, guided by the clanking of chains, they again came in sight of the ghost, which as suddenly disappeared as if the earth had swallowed it up.

But Tom was not to be hoodwinked. Proceeding to the spot, he found a hole, and introducing his hand, first drew out a large turnip lantern, fashioned like a skull with a still warm candle in it. Next he drew out the white-sheeted tenant of the farm, the chains having been dropped in the hole. Then Tom began with the ash plant... and the shrieks of the ghost were fearful on the still morning air. The Old Hall Dobby was never seen or heard again. ❄

** Bogey – Another term for a boggle, or ghost.*

† Crossing the sands – Crossing Morecambe Bay (usually from Hest Bank, Lancashire to Kents Bank, Cumbria) was a shortcut that could save travellers heading into the Lake District many hours, but it was treacherous because of the quicksands and tide. Many lives have been lost making the trip over the centuries.

THE CRIER OF CLAIFE

THE Crier of Claife is unique in British ghost lore as the only spirit marked on the maps of the Ordnance Survey. Its haunted home is a woodland grove on the west bank of Windermere.

'The Kendal Mercury', 25 December, 1852.

MUCH as this district of ours is searched by travellers, and explored by guidebook makers, there are many rare and interesting nooks that, if sought for with grateful hearts, could not fail to yield much pleasure if cheerfully accepted, and some old corners – interwoven with legendary lore and strange associations – that have not yet found an historian. The Crier of Claife is one of them.

The ancient festival of Christmas, being the time when people in country places gather round a fire and feed their imaginations with scraps of old legends and tales of local boggles and ghosts that haunt their native hills and dells, was an inducement to entice us to our wild old wandering ground. We early imbibed a strong relish for tales of ghosts and haunted places, and had a most sincere attachment for the place that heads this article, and often as opportunity would allow, wandered thither, much to the annoyance of the moor birds and scattered black-faced sheep, whose silent domain we were intruding on. But we always imagined that a ramble on the haunted hill refreshed our feelings and thoughts.

Before we speak of the Crier, a word or two about the township of Claife. Claife is a division of Hawkshead parish, situated between the lakes of Windermere and Esthwaite, and contains about

4,500 acres of land. The whole townships includes 89 houses, and, according to the census returns of last year, the population was 551.

Upwards of three centuries ago – the time from which the place we are to talk about dates its hauntedness – Claife was a poor, badly cultivated district, greatly overgrown with wood, and anything but favourable for agriculture. But the population began to increase, and the wants of the inhabitants increased also, and the woodman's axe awoke the echoes that had before only echoed to the hunter's shout. It has now become rather a smart region, far from behind in cultivation.

The Crier, with its unenviable reputation of being haunted, is situated on a wild and lonely eminence in the middle of the townships, in the midst of the plantations of Henry Curwen Esq., about a mile-and-a-half up the hill from Waterloo Gardens on the banks of Windermere, seemingly cut off from the busy haunts of man. The most prominent object at the place is an old quarry, from which the flags and slates that adorn the old class of houses in the township were quarried.

If it be visited in summer time, the surrounding view is most magnificent; the visitor may see the whole length and breadth of Windermere, stretching in loveliness at one view, and on fine evenings it is a delightful place – a place on which, when the sun does shine, it seems to shine more pleasantly than elsewhere, lighting up the slopes and lake in a flood of golden light. But in winter it is a desolate landscape, secluded from the noise of trade and bustle of everyday life – no sound to break the solitude, no sign of human life, and it is not possible to visit the place in mid-winter without being awestruck with the overpowering loneliness of the scene.

It may be from superstitious motives, but so it is that we never gaze on the dreary place but a thrill of awe comes over our mind, and it is in vain we try to realise in all their bearing the traditional associations awakened thereby.

Everything like clear evidence – of course – is gone, save the rude old quarry, and the tradition is transmitted from one generation to another by no more secure vehicle than oral communication.

There are two things we are certain of and thankful for, namely that we never saw a ghost ourselves, and that there are people who have, and we are under a particular debt of gratitude to those who have a vision for the invisible, for this Christmas would limp on very tediously and this ghost story of ours would never have been told but for such keen-sighted folks.

How Claife became home to the Crier is detailed in the continuing narrative below. The ghost story originates in the days when villagers from Sawrey on the west shore of Windermere would call out for a ferryman stationed at The Nab near Bowness when they required passage over the lake.

IT was a wild stormy night about Martinmas, somewhere about 330 years ago, when a shout across The Nab called the ferry boatman from amongst a lot of roystering travellers that had taken up their quarters at the-then humble alehouse, sheltering from the inclemency of the weather and furious storm that raged out of doors.

When sufficient time had elapsed for the boatman to return, the half-drunken guests staggered to the landing to see who the newcomer might be – for in those days travellers were few – but the boatman had returned alone; a sober, silent man, with terror marked in every feature of his face.

He was with difficulty got to bed, and awoke next morning in a violent fever, that carried him off in a few days, but he never could be prevailed upon to say a word of what had befallen him at The Nab. For weeks after, when the weather was boisterous, there were eager and violent shoutings and cries at The Nab, but the story of the apparition had got noised abroad, so that no boatman could be found that dared to venture across the lake after dark.

These times were the days of abbeys and convents, and the Cistercian monks held sway and ruled Furness fells from the Abbey of Saint Mary in Furness, and a monk or friar used to attend the little convent on Chapel Island, half-a-mile north of Bowness Bay, to ease the inhabitants of the district of their sins and money. To him was application made about the dreaded Nab affair.

These monasteries, founded at first as the abodes of piety and letters and refuges for the desolate and penitent, had become the haunts of idleness and superstition. Ready – very ready – were the monks to comply with the request of the neighbourhood to remove the ghost, on condition that a certain amount of money was forthcoming when the incantation was completed, for in those days, as in our own times, amongst the Roman Catholics there was 'no penny, no paternoster'. As to the exact year in which the ceremony was performed, all is left in doubt and dimmest twilight, but there is every certainty that it was Christmas Day when the monks and their attendants met the zealous inhabitants of the thinly-populated district on Chapel Island.

In the sacerdotal performance there was much rhapsody and little sober reason or religion – very much that was calculated to inflame the inexperienced imagination, but little that could direct the erring judgement. It was a sad spectacle for half-a-dozen cowled monks to persuade many hundred people they possessed power over supernatural things. But it was an age of faith, and the whole multitude left the island firmly believing that henceforth and forever 'The Nab flay' must take up its location at the Crier. Since then, centuries have passed away, and not a name exists of any individual that took part in the solemn service.

The district is now busy – far busier than in those days. The simple inhabitants of the township then are far, far away; the veteran souls of many centuries. We might tell how that, in times past, the fox-hounds, when in full chase, often came to a stand at the place that had become the dwelling place of ghosts without anyone being able to assign the reason; and of a schoolmaster from Colthouse who, within the present generation, left home one evening to go past the spot, but was never seen or heard of more; and many other mysterious tales of people being mightily terrified... but time and space will not permit.

Some will be ready to exclaim that these old prejudices are swept away; that we have shaken off the trammels of ancient delusion, and folk do not believe in the imps of darkness now. But really the writer never knew an individual who visited the place in twilight without confessing to a heart-clutching fear of unearthly company. And perhaps at the very moment this is being read, the whole multitude of ghostly beings may be holding their anniversary Christmas revel at the Crier. We will now let our readers go to bed, wishing them a very merry, happy Christmas, and they may make as many reflections as they please on our humble district narrative. ❄

CASTLERIGG GHOST

Boggles often pre-empted tragedy. Such was the case in this account of a ghostly horse that rode near Keswick. The tale was first recorded in a letter from Miss Frances Rolleston in 1853.

'The Letters of Miss Frances Rolleston of Keswick',*
compiled Caroline Dent, 1867.

Keswick, 26 December, 1853.

My Dearest Cary, I am afraid you know so little of this country, that you neither know Rake Foot lonely farm-house, nor Joseph Summers' on Castlerigg, both far in the wild, on the left hand as you descend the Ambleside hill. But figure to yourself the rocky cleft, with its rushing torrent, Rake Foot, by its side. There lived a fine young mountaineer who courted a mountain girl at Joseph Summers' just below. He was a sober, well-conducted young man, but we cannot find that he attended any place of worship, or gave any signs of religious impressions.

Driving one night towards Cockermouth for lime, his horse started. He looked round and saw on the other side of the hedge the figure of a great tall horse. It kept abreast of him, 'louping along' for a mile-and-a-half. He was in a state of terror the whole time, and with continual returns of that terror told to many persons what he had seen – which of course is now the talk of the country.

He went miles round to avoid that part of the road for three weeks that followed this visitation until his death.

It was on Christmas eve he lingered about till midnight in the hopes of seeing his girl. He was then seen to go homewards, but it is supposed that knowing his family were afraid of night alarms, he would not knock them up, but made himself a bed under the manger of the horse he was accustomed to drive.

In the morning the boy called to him – but he did not move. A light was brought. He had moved from under the manger to the side of the horse, and it had lain down on him and crushed him to death.

– *Miss Frances Rolleston.*

* Frances Rolleston (1781–1864) is best known for her book *Mazzaroth: the Constellations* in which she "presents readers with her theory of 'the gospel in the stars'". Rolleston believed that through the ancient names for the stars you could discover the oldest knowledge transmitted from God to man: "the method of man's redemption and the coming of the Jewish messiah". Even in their time, these were unusual ideas that never gained much ground, but Rolleston achieved much in her life for good. Born in London in 1781, she joined the evangelical movement at a young age and was involved in the emancipation of slaves and fundraising for wounded soldiers in the Crimean War. She visited the Lake District in 1847 and was so impressed that she moved to Keswick the following year. She spent her time writing, painting and performing good works in the town. She died at the age of 83 and is buried in the churchyard at St John's in the Vale.

A year after her death a fountain was erected in Keswick commemorating her work for the town's poor. It was restored in 2000 and can be found on Station Road adjacent to Fitz Park.

THE SLAVER IN THE SOLWAY

STAND on the west coast of Cumbria on Christmas Eve, it is said, and you may see the ghost ship Betsey-Jane, endeavouring to reach Whitehaven harbour. The story behind her doomed journey was recorded in 1873 by John Pagen White.

'Lays & Legends of the English Lake Country', J. P. White, 1873.

WHEN Whitehaven-born John Pagen White wrote this ballad in 1873, he was almost certainly basing it on an existing legend of a ghost ship that sailed on the Solway every Christmas, but he took the legend and turned it into a piece of anti-slavery propaganda – in support of a cause he supported.

The Betsey-Jane sailed out of the Firth,
As the waits sang "Christ is born on earth" –
The Betsey-Jane sailed out of the Firth,
On Christmas-day in the morning.

The wind was east, the moon was high,
Of a frosty blue was the spangled sky,
And the bells were ringing, and dawn was nigh,
And the day was Christmas morning.

In village and town woke up from sleep,
From peaceful visions and slumbers deep –
In village and town woke up from sleep,
On Christmas-day in the morning.

The many that thought on Christ the King,
And rose betimes their gifts to bring,
And 'peace on earth and good will' to sing,
As is meet upon Christmas morning.

The Betsey-Jane pass'd village and town,
As the Gleemen* sang, and the stars went down –
The Betsey-Jane pass'd village and town,
That Christmas-day in the morning;

And the Skipper by good and by evil swore,
The bells might ring and the Gleemen roar,
But the chink of his gold would chime him o'er
Those waves, next Christmas morning.

And out of the Firth with his reckless crew,
All ready his will and his work to do –
Out of the Firth with his reckless crew
He sailed on a Christmas morning!

He steer'd his way to Gambia's coast;
And dealt for slaves; and Westward cross'd;
And sold their lives, and made his boast
As he thought upon Christmas morning.

And again and again from shore to shore,
With his human freight for the golden ore –
Again and again from shore to shore,
Ere Christmas-day in the morning.

He cross'd that deep with never a thought
Of the sorrow, or wrong, or suffering wrought,
On souls and bodies thus sold and bought
For gold, against Christmas morning!

And at length, with his gold and ivory rare,
When the sun was low and the breeze was fair –
At length with his gold and ivory rare
He sailed, that on Christmas morning.

He might pass both village and town again
When the bells were ringing, as they rung then,
When he pass'd them by in the Betsey-Jane,
On that last bright Christmas morning.

The Betsey-Jane sailed into the Firth,
As the bells rang 'Christ is born on earth' –
The Betsey-Jane sailed into the Firth,
And it was upon Christmas morning!

The wind was west, the moon was high,
Of a hazy blue was the spangled sky,
And the bells were ringing, and dawn was nigh,
Just breaking on Christmas morning.

The Gleemen singing of Christ the King,
Of Christ the King, of Christ the King –
The Gleemen singing of Christ the King,
Hailed Christmas-day in the morning;

When the Betsey-Jane with a thundering shock
Went ripping along on the Giltstone Rock†,
In sound of the bells which seemed to mock
Her doom on that Christmas morning.

With curse and shriek and fearful groan,
On the foundering ship, in the waters lone –
With curse and shriek and fearful groan,
They sank on that Christmas morning!

The Skipper with arms around his gold,
Scared by dark spirits that loosed his hold,
Was down the deep sea plunged and roll'd
In the dawn of that Christmas morning:

While village and town woke up from sleep,
From peaceful visions and slumbers deep –
While village and town woke up from sleep,
That Christmas-day in the morning!

And many that thought on Christ the King,
Rose up betimes their gifts to bring,
And 'peace on earth and goodwill to sing,'
Went forth in the Christmas morning! ❄

* *Gleemen – An old term for minstrels.*

† *Giltstone Rock lies north of Whitehaven.*

PART 3

SNOW & NATURE

THE GREAT FROST OF 1895

FEBRUARY 1895 saw the 'Great Frost' descend on Britain. The Lake District experienced it more than most. Windermere was frozen across its entire length, the ice 18 inches thick in places. This led to much merriment on the lake and excited reports in local and national papers.

'The Shields Gazette', 18 February, 1895.

Twenty Thousand People Skating on Windermere

THE scene on Windermere Lake on Saturday, when 15,000 to 20,000 people were on the ice, was one never to be forgotten by those who witnessed it. The Lake is frozen from end to end, 12 to 13 miles, with a single break at the ferry kept open for the ferry steamer, which connects the Kendal and Hawkshead highway. The ice is smooth as glass, and 1ft to 18in thick.

The Furness Railway Company's steam yachts* have been frozen for some weeks. The London and North-western, Midland, and Furness Railway Companies have offered cheap facilities to the public, and thousands of people have thronged to the lake from far and near. All the big towns and cities, including London, have sent large contingents of visitors, with the result that all hotels and private lodging houses are even more crowded than in the height of the summer season. This means a rich harvest to the district if the frost holds out long.

From the summit of Biscay Howe, above Bowness – a vantage ground which commands a view the Lake almost for its entire length – the scene Saturday was one to be ever remembered. A perfect sheet of ice was seen north and south, dotted over either with skaters or with sleighs drawn by otherwise 'unemployed' men. The greatest life and mirth was evinced, and everybody seemed to enjoy the novel experience. The hills all round are covered with snow. Skaters report the ice exceedingly good.

'The Westminster Gazette', 21 February, 1895.

Skating on Windermere

THERE are some scenes of natural beauty that, besides affording the keenest enjoyment at the time, leave in the mind of the observer a memory and picture which it is always a pleasure to revive and dwell upon. A sunrise on the slopes of Mount Blanc or the early-morning moonlight on some 'spectral glacier' of the Oberland are pictures that rest in the mind's eye long after the originals have faded. Similarly, a day on the frozen surface of Windermere is an experience to treasure among many other remembrances of the Great Frost of February, 1895.

We found Lakeside busy with skaters, while the snow-covered hills were reflected as in a mirror, in a perfect sheet of hard black ice. Fairfield and Loughrigg glowed far away in a rosy Alpine sunset, and slowly faded away into a livid white. As night fell, the great stars shone still and bright in the icy lake, while the great water – after the hot February sunshine – went to rest with loud cracks that boomed from shore to shore as though the spirit of the lake were trying to escape from its frozen prison.

Gradually the skaters departed, until we were left the only guests of the comfortable Lakeside Hotel. We went out in the starlight and waited for the moon to rise over the hills. Far into the night we could hear the ice cracking and roaring in the stillness.

Wednesday, 13 February opened with a hazy sunrise, intensely cold. We started about ten o'clock – five of us, including two ladies, to skate up the lake to Waterhead. Distances were lost in a silver haze, and although we found tracks on the ice, and occasionally saw other wanderers, we could almost imagine with the Ancient Mariner, that 'we were the first that ever burst into that silent sea'.

We skirted the eastern shore for about two miles, sometimes skating over shoal water, knee-deep, where through the thin transparent ice we could see the pebbles at the bottom and frightened minnows flying from our shadows. Some of the ice here – which bore perfectly – could not have been more than an inch thick, and some even less.

A great stretch of strong black ice brought us to Storrs Hall, and soon we were at Bowness Ferry, where, as the ferry-boat was running, we had to land for a few yards. Bowness Bay was like a London park – an ice yacht was being fitted out, and later we heard that a tandem sleigh had been driven round it. Passing out between the islands, we stretched across for the western shore at Wray. On each side of the track lay fields of smooth black ice, where little flocks of wild ducks were obliged to rest. As we neared the head of the lake, the High Street and Helvellyn ranges shone white above a rising haze.

A stream that runs in above Wray Castle causes a crack which extends right across to the further shore, but we easily turned it by keeping well in-shore, and creeping under the islands crowned with Scotch fir that screen the mouth of the Brathay. We reached Waterhead Pier at noon – an easy two hours' run.

Whilst so many pieces of ice have been spoilt by snow this winter, Windermere did not freeze until after the snow, so that there was a stretch of ice some 11 miles long, averaging, say, three-quarters of a mile in width, which for extent and quality would be very hard to beat, even in the Engadin. As a study in ice structure, it afforded a great opportunity for a scientist: the tenacity of ice frozen at a low temperature could be tested, while at Wray there were several acres of ice covered with an erect fan-like growth of thin, brittle white ice standing up about three inches from the surface, which I have never seen explained. But, just as in climbing one forgets the claims of geology, so here we welcomed the black glassy surface without inquiring too closely into its structure. ❄

* *Before Windermere Lake Cruises, there were Furness Railway Company's steam yachts.*

WASTWATER FROZEN

IT wasn't just Windermere that froze during the Great Frost. Further west, even Wastwater – deepest of the lakes – was undergoing an unprecedented freeze.

'The Whitehaven News', 21 February, 1895.

THE frost continues to hold the country in firm grip. Some days during the week, the power of the mid-day sun sets the snow and ice melting in exposed places, and a good deal has thus disappeared where the drainage is good. But every evening the frost has got hold with a fresh grip, and the nights have been severe, making the roads dangerous to travellers. Yesterday there was word from Wasdale that the lake there was nearly covered by a thin sheet of ice. This is an occurrence unprecedented. Mr Musgrave at that time went on the lake for the express purpose of trying the temperature, and found that at a depth of 20ft it was six degrees short of freezing point.

Wastwater, as is well known, is a very deep lake, and thus requires a prolonged exposure to a low temperature before it can all be cooled down to the point of greatest density and thus freeze. There must be some other cause than that of mere depth, however, to account for Wastwater not generally freezing. Its greatest depth is 280 feet. Windermere is not far short of it, with a greatest depth of 240 feet, yet Windermere has been frozen for some time, and is a sort of national skating rink just now. ❄

SKATING ON DERWENT WATER

Skating on the frozen lakes and tarns of Lakeland was common during the longer, colder winters of Cumbria past. Numerous writers chronicle the pastime – including both William and Dorothy Wordsworth – and a pair of skates would be found in many a home and farmhouse. In the excerpt below, National Trust co-founder Hardwicke Rawnsley captures the atmosphere of a Keswick winter, and of skating alone on Derwent Water at dawn.

'Chapters at the English Lakes', Canon H. D. Rawnsley, 1913.

NOTHING could have been more magical than the afterglow last Sunday evening upon Skiddaw and Helvellyn. Ere the rose-red faded from their snow-clad heights, there swam up into sight between Latrigg and Wanthwaite the moon, a little past its full, shining like a great oval jewel in a cup of liquid amethyst – that eastern cup of winter sky from which we folk in the Keswick valley on these clear evenings drink our full of wonder and surprise. Within half-an-hour of moonrise Orion stood up huge in the south-western sky, Syrius sparkled above Walla Crag, and the Plough was clear above Old Skiddaw's cone. The stillness of a Sabbath possessed the vale, until from wood to wood the owls hooted cheerily, and dogs answered each other at distant farms.

I had heard in the late afternoon the tremulous metallic murmur of skaters [on the lake]. The sound of organ and hymn came faintly from the old church of St Kentigern, then the patter of many feet along the road for home, and deeper silence fell on hill and Dale. I knew that tomorrow, if the wind kept in the east, the ice on Derwent Water would be in prime condition, and having much work to do, I also knew that there would be no skating for me unless rising betimes I could go off by star and moonlight to the lake.

At five-thirty I was astir. Great silver clouds built up the heights of nobler mountains in the south, but westward the moon shone in a cloudless sky. Leaving the quiet house and passing through the sleeping hamlet and through the little town, which, but for light in three windows and in the pencil factory, was still asleep, I made my way to the lake, and as the clock struck six – the only living thing in that strange landscape – I shod myself with steel, and struck out from the land.

Orion had sunk beneath the western hills; the Plough was at the zenith. I knew that three morning stars were rejoicing together to run their course, but one was not yet visible above the hills, the other was dimmed by the moonlight that seemed to wash the heaven clear of stars save where Cassiopeia still sparkled faintly above Skiddaw and Jupiter, rejoicing in his strength and glory, yet shone clear above Scafell. As I saw it gleam in the polished ice, I could not help thinking of how Wordsworth years ago on Esthwaite Lake* had seen just such reflection of a planet when he cut across the reflex of a star.

The weirdness of the scene lay in the fact that all the near hills seemed blackened as though the breath of a great fire had passed over them and left behind white ash and ebon darkness. The woods about the lake appeared to have grown in density. One might have supposed Derwent Water stood in a huge forest; in the dim moonlight the dark woods seemed so magnified in mass. There was no sound of life except the bark of dogs from the neighbouring town and the calling of the owls to one another across the lake. There was no sight of life except that in two or three places in the dense woodland a bright lamp shone that told us that the busy servants of the household were awake.

It was poorish skating, for though brooms had been busy on Saturday, the ice had been much cut by skates, and on beyond this broomland the snow of Thursday lay in patches. Beyond the white snow patches lay what looked at first in the dim twilight like open water. It was not till I was close above it that I found this open water a solid sheet of ice without a wrinkle in it. I hissed across that wonderful ice-sheet, swerving and curving with a sense of unaccustomed speed, with Jupiter bright in the mirror before me and the great moon pillar of gold across my way, till, out of breath, and with the blood racing warm through my heart, I leaned upon my heels and let the wind carry me where it would.

But the beauty was not in heaven, but upon the shining ebon floor of the lake. Its dark blackness disappeared, and in a moment the vast ice sheet became first green, then gold, and then of rosy hue. Involuntarily I pulled up and gazed upon the wonder thus revealed, and as I gazed the wonder grew and grew. The moon was still shining above Hindscarth, the sun had not yet appeared, but all her light had paled before the coming of the day, and all the mystery of the heavens was forgotten in the marvel of that polished floor of rose and gold ingrain.

It is good to skate at noon and eventide. It is better far to skate when moon and starlight fade before the dawn. ❄

* *A reference to Wordsworth's autobiographical poem 'The Prelude', which recalls boyhood skating expeditions on Esthwaite Water during his time at Hawkshead School.*

A WALK ON ICED ENNERDALE

MORE Great Frost revelry is described at a busy Ennerdale Water, where locals walk to the island and tragedy is averted as a youngster is pulled from the ice.

'Carlisle Journal', 21 February, 1895.

SKATING has been going on continually on Ennerdale Lake during the past week. Conveyances of all descriptions have been going through the village with skaters. At the Anglers' Inn* the scene was like that of a busy day in summer. On Sunday last a thaw somewhat spoiled the surface of the ice on the side nearest the Inn, but under Crag Fell, where the sun does not shine, the ice is in as good a condition as ever.

Many persons walked to the island in the centre of the lake† on Sunday out of curiosity. Mr A. Wilson of Whitehaven has taken some views of the lake with skaters &c. So far we have heard of no serious accidents. On Saturday morning a little girl named Mary Barker got in the ice on the River Ehen up to the neck. She was along with a companion, Martha Ray, who promptly handed her a long stick and helped her out. Fortunately, she has not suffered from her cold bath. ❄

* *The Angler's Inn – that overlooked the lake at its outflow – was demolished in 1961.*
† *At times of low water levels, islands emerge between Bowness and Anglers Crag.*

A FROSTY CHRISTMAS DAY, 1836

We have plenty of records of snow in historic Christmas diaries, but few accounts are as detailed as those maintained by Whitehaven meteorologist John Fletcher Miller – who also notes the tardy delivery time of the seasonal post.

'The diary of John Fletcher Miller', 1836.

A MORE beautifully clear and settled evening than the last we never witnessed. Not the smallest cloud bedimmed the Azure Arch of Heaven, and the moon – one day past the full – shone through a serene and exceedingly sharp, frosty atmosphere. During the night we had a fall of snow, for at 8a.m. this morning the ground was covered to the depth of 1¼ inches on average, and at 9a.m. the thermometer stood at 23 degrees.

The day has been generally clear, with frequent sudden snowy showers that sometimes formed almost instantaneously, and with scarcely any visible cloud. It has been by far the coldest day we have had within the limit of my observations, its mean temperature being 24.4 degrees. The barometer has been unaffected by this change. In consequence of the snow, the mail did not arrive till 2 p.m.

THE SNOW

John Richardson (1817–1886) was a dialect poet who lived all his life in Naddle, near Keswick. He is buried at St John's church above St John's in the Vale, where you can find a small exhibition devoted to Naddle valley's most famous resident.

John Richardson, 1876.

It com doon as whisht an' as deftly as death,
O' soond nut a murmur, o' air nut a breath;
Flake reacin' wi' flake. Oh ! 'twas bonny to see
Hoo it cuvver't up moontain, an' valley, an' tree.
Doon, doon it com floatin', sa' white an' sa clear,
Ivvery twig, ivvery leaf, hed its burden to bear;
Ivvery dyke, ivvery hoose, ivvery rough cobble wo',
Hed its blossom, its reuf, or its copin' o' snow.
Doon, doon it com' floatin' sa' swiftly an' leet,
Seun t' landscape was white as a tribble bleach't sheet;
An' t' grund 'at was leatly sa' starv't like an' bare,
Was lapt in a mantle, a feut thick or mair,
Their coald stores exhaustit, t' leet cloods floatit by,
An' pure white as t' earth was, as deep blue was t' sky;
Far sooth Sol* appeared, majestic an' breet,
His rays wake an' slantin', an' guiltless o' heat,
Threw ower that white picter a splendour an' sheen,
'At twice in a life-time can rarely be seen.
Ivvery crag, ivvery dyke, ivvery snow-leaden tree,
Was an object worth gaan a lang journey to see;
Neah art, tho' by t' cleverest artist, could show
A picter sa' grand as that landscape o' snow.

T' grim demon o' winter, wi' envy hofe craz'd,
To see sec a scene i' December – uprais't
A fierce wind fra t' north, 'at whissel't an' rwoar't,
An' dreav t' snow i' blinndin' cloods dancin' afwore 't.
Fra t' fells into t' valleys, doon whurlin' it went,
It fand ivvery crack, ivvery crevice, an' rent;
Through t' mortarless wo's; in auld hooses, it's sed,
Fwok waken't to finnd theirsels snown up i' bed.
While creelin' by t' fences for shelter, t' poor sheep,
In t' snowdrifts war hap't up, aye, ivver sa' deep;
For days an' days efter, t' auld shipperds wad post
Off wi' t' cwollies, to hunt up odd sheep 'at war lost;
An' some nivver fund war till spring, when leate on
They frozen turn't oot efter t' last snow was gone!

* *Sol – Sun.*

THE STORM

WE pretend to hate the disruption wrought by heavy snowfall. But we like nothing more than to talk about it...

'Whitehaven News', 14 February, 1895.

THE snow storm of last week was one of exceptional severity with us, exceeding any experienced by the oldest inhabitants, and this not only from the depth of snow, but from the fierce and bitterly cold wind accompanying it. Those who were unfortunately compelled to face it will long remember it as a most trying experience.

In our district there were several instances of men almost frozen to death from exposure on the Wednesday night, but in every case they were fortunate in reaching shelter when in the last extremity.

The heavy drifts of snow on our roads made traffic impossible until men were employed to remove them. This had also to be done on our railway, which was completely blocked, and could not run until Saturday, causing a delay of two days in the delivery and despatch of letters.

The popular concert of the Eskdale Fox Hunt had to be postponed last Friday in consequence of the snow. It is hoped this will have no injurious effect upon the attendance on the 22nd now fixed.

SNOW PROBLEM

FOLK through the ages have delighted in the first dusting of snow. But get too much – and the complaints soon begin. It's a phenemenon wryly noted in the *Wigton Advertiser* way back in 1860.

'Wigton Advertiser', 7 January, 1860.

EVERY freezable thing has been frozen. In the morning – if not frozen to your sheets – you find your jug, basin and water all in one lump, your sponge like a stone, and window like a sheet of ice... the very bread frozen, and your leg of mutton like petrifaction. The cups and saucers froze together in one house we know of. Gas meters that never froze before congealed and 'put out their pipes' with a vengeance, refusing even the inspiriting administration of a gill of whisky given inwardly – a favourite cure. Shops looked dismal. The lights 'burned blue'* or did not burn at all. Candles, oil-lamps and paraffin had to be resorted to.

The country looks most winter-like in its clothing of snow. The marsh is frozen, the river dead. Birds are almost starved, and will scarcely take the trouble of flying out of your way in walking in the country. In short, it is just such weather as we have been wishing for when complaining of the mildness of our seasons, and now, when we have it, we find it anything but a welcome visitor. ❄

** Likely a reference to the fuel burning as well as it could in the cold. Gas burning blue is using up all the oxygen.*

ANDERSON'S ROBIN

Is there anything that heralds Christmas more than a robin's song? The bird's curiosity and lack of timidness when snatching a crumb from human hand has melted even the coldest hearts. It is the bird's loyalty that appealed to Cumberland dialect poet Robert Anderson – particularly after being forsaken by his 'bonny bit' sweetheart.

'Ballads in the Cumberland Dialect', Robert Anderson, 1808.

'AT six o'clock on the snowy morning of 1 February, 1770, I first beheld the light of this world at the Damn Side in the suburbs of the ancient city of Carlisle." So wrote Robert Anderson – often known as The Cumberland Bard – in his autobiography. He was born to a poor family, but received education from the Quakers. His ballad 'The Redbreest' was inspired by a robin that visited him each year for five years. "He commonly gave me his first cheerful strain in the beginning of September; and sang his farewell to the noise and smoke of the town in April. So tame was the merry minstrel that he frequently made a hearty repast within a few inches from the paper on which I wrote."

It is said that Anderson returned to Carlisle after a long absence and overheard 'The Redbreest' being sung in a Castle Street pub. He broke down in tears on hearing it was still popular after so many years. The bard was at home with fellow rustics, but he also counted William Wordsworth among his supporters. Anderson died in 1833 and a public monument was erected by subscription to his memory. It stands in the grounds of Carlisle Cathedral. ❄

THE REDBREEST

Come into my cabin, red Robin!
Threyce welcome, lal warbler, to me!
Now Skiddaw he's thrown his wheyte cap on,
Agean I'll gi'e shelter to thee.

Just hop thy ways into my pantry,
And feast on my peer humble fare;
I never was fash'd wid a dainty,
But meyne, man or bird, sal ay share.

Now four years are by-geane, red Robin,
Sin furst thou com singin' to me;
But, how, how I's chang'd, little Robin,
Sin furst I bade welcome to thee!

I then had a bonny bit lassie,
Away wid anudder she's geane;
My frien's wad oft caw at my cabin,
Now dowie I seegh aw my leane.

Oh, where is thy sweetheart, red Robin?
Gae bring her frae house-top or tree;
I'll bid her be true to sweet Robin,
For fause was lassie to me.

You'll share ev'ry crumb i' my cabin,
We'll sing the cauld winter away;
I wunnet deceive ye, peer burdies!
Let mortals use me as they may.

TO A REDBREAST (IN SICKNESS)

Sara Hutchinson (1779–1835), sister of Wordsworth's wife Mary, died from consumption aged 54 at Rydal Mount near Grasmere. As she lay on her sick bed in January 1826 she was comforted by visits from a robin.

'The Poetical Words of William Wordsworth', 1882.

STAY, little cheerful Robin! stay,
And at my casement sing,
Though it would prove a farewell lay
And this our parting spring.
Though I, alas! may ne'er enjoy
The promise in thy song;
A charm, that thought can not destroy,
Doth to thy strain belong.
Methinks that in my dying hour
Thy song would still be dear,
And with a more than earthly power
My passing Spirit cheer.
Then, little Bird, this boon confer,
Come, and my requiem sing,
Nor fail to be the harbinger
Of everlasting Spring.

THE 'BIRD THAT NEVER FLEW'

Long associated with folklore, a once-loved robin was bought back from the dead by St Mungo, Keswick's patron saint, as one of four miracles.

NO place in Cumbria is associated more closely with the robin than Keswick. The bird is linked with the town through its patron saint, St Kentigern, often known by his 'pet' name of St Mungo ('my dear one'), who came to Keswick in 553 AD. There are four miracles associated with Mungo, remembered in the following verse:

Here is the bird that never flew
Here is the tree that never grew
Here is the bell that never rang
Here is the fish that never swam.

The 'bird that never flew' was a pet robin that belonged to St Serf, leader at the monastery at Culross in Fife, which gave sanctuary to Mungo and his mother. The bird was killed by young boys at Culross, but Mungo miraculously brought it back to life.

The 'tree that never grew' refers to another legend associated with the monastery at Culross. Mungo was in charge of keeping the flames of a holy fire at the monastery lit, but while he slept jealous rivals put the flame out. Mungo blew on a branch of hazel, which burst into flames and re-ignited the sacred fire.

The 'bell that never rang' refers to a bell Mungo brought back from Rome and which was used in services to mourn the dead.

And the 'fish'? This relates to Mungo's help gifted to the sixth century Queen of Strathclyde, who was accused by the King of infidelity. He demanded to see the ring he had given her as a lover's token. She was unable to find it (in fact the King had secretly stolen it himself and thrown it into the Clyde). She was facing execution, but Mungo ordered a messenger to catch a fish in the river. On cutting into the fish's flesh, the ring was miraculously found inside, and the Queen was able to clear her name.

If you visit St Kentigern's church at Crosthwaite, look out for the robin, tree, fish and bell symbols that recall his four miracles – they can all be found in a mosaic on the floor of the church. ❄

SNOW PANCAKES

NORTHERN cooks have long used snow as a secret ingredient in winter-time pancakes. Ruth, Mike and the Williamson family have farmed at Crosby Ravensworth in Westmorland for 40 years. When snow falls, it's time to heat the frying pan for the local delicacy...

From the blog of Ruth Tuer of Crake Trees Manor Farm, 2017.

AT Crake Trees we had a proper snowfall last night and woke up to the beautiful silence and sunshine that surrounds the countryside for a short time on that first morning of winter snow. The sheep are happy, the horses want to be out straight away without rugs, and the Jack Russells go mad rolling over and over in the snow. Apart from all exposed water pipes being frozen at the cattle sheds, life seems good.

The grandsons Bill and Ted wanted to make pancakes for supper. The snow is crisp but fluffy, and just right for that important task of being the premier ingredient in snow pancakes. What is it about the snow? Who thought of using snow in the pancake mix? I don't know, but the pancakes certainly taste wonderful and have a strange texture that the frozen air molecules create.

When following my recipe, be careful where you gather your snow – avoid areas where dogs have been..!

We had the snow pancakes with leftover rum butter *(page 135)* from Christmas and a squirt of lemon to sharpen them a little. ☞

SNOW PANCAKES
INGREDIENTS

Makes six snow pancakes.

- 4 1/2oz plain flour.
- 4 1/2oz spelt flour (if no spelt flour available, use 9oz plain flour).
- 4 medium eggs.
- 2oz melted butter.
- Vanilla essence, one drop.
- Milk, half pint.
- Fresh snow*, half pint.

RECIPE

- Mix the flour with the beaten eggs and melted butter, then add a drop of vanilla essence.
- With a wooden spoon, slowly beat in the milk and then the snow.
- With a knob of butter or teaspoon of vegetable oil, grease a frying pan. Apply a medium heat until the fat melts.
- Add enough batter to thinly cover the surface of the pan. When bubbles appear in the pancake, flip it and cook the other side.
- When cooked, stack the pancakes and keep covered.

Notes:

– The first pancake is the cook's perk, which can be eaten whilst the second is cooking.

*– * You can cheat and use sparkling water instead of snow. A good glug of local ale has also been added to the mix in the past!*

THE CHILDREN ON THE FELLS

Winter tragedies on the fells are all too common. In 1807, Sarah and George Green succumbed to a snow storm as they returned from a furniture sale in Great Langdale to their children at Blentarn Ghyll, Easedale. Trapped in the family smallholding by snow, the children waited days for news of their parents before sounding the alarm. The parents' bodies were eventually found on the fell. One of the children was a domestic help at the home of William Wordsworth, who helped raise funds for the orphans. The children's tale was told by Wordsworth's friend Thomas de Quincey.

'The Golden Gift', Thomas de Quincey, 1868.

THE eldest sister, little Agnes, though sadly alarmed, and feeling the sensation of eeriness as twilight came on, yet exerted herself to take all the measures which their own prospects made prudent.

Having caused all her brothers and sisters except the two little things (not yet of a fit age) to kneel down and say the prayers which they had been taught, this admirable little maiden turned herself to every household task that could have proved useful to them in a long captivity. First of all, upon some recollection that the clock was nearly going down, she wound it up. Next, she took all the milk which remained from what her mother had provided for the children's consumption during her absence and scalded it, so as to save it from turning sour.

That done, she next examined the meal chest, made the common oatmeal porridge of the country, and put all of the children, except the two youngest, on short allowance; then, by way of reconciling them in some measure to this stinted meal, she found a little hoard of flour, part of which she baked for them upon the hearth into little cakes. This unusual delicacy persuaded them to think that they had been celebrating a feast.

Next, before night coming on should make it too trying, or before fresh snow coming on might make it impossible, she issued out of doors. There her first task was, with the assistance of two younger brothers, to carry in from the peat-stack as many peats as might serve them for a week. That done, in the second place she examined the potatoes, buried in brackens: these were not many, and she thought it better to leave them where they were, excepting as many as would make a single meal, under a fear that the heat of their cottage would spoil them if removed.

Having thus made all the provision in her power for supporting their own lives, she turned her attention to the cow. Her she milked; but unfortunately the milk she gave – either from being badly fed or from some other cause – was too trifling to be of much consideration towards the wants of a large family. Her chief anxiety was to get down the hay for the cow's food from a loft above the outhouse. In this she succeeded, but imperfectly, from want of strength and size to cope with the difficulties of the case – besides that the increasing darkness by this time, together with the gloom of the place, made it a matter of great self-conquest for her to work at all. But, as respected one night at any rate, she placed the cow in a situation of luxurious warmth and comfort.

Then retreating into the warm house, and barring the door, she sat down to undress the two youngest of the children: them she laid carefully and cosily in their little nests upstairs, and saw them to sleep. The rest she kept up to bear her company until the clock should tell them it was midnight; up to which time she had a lingering hope that some welcome shout from the hills above, which they were all to strain their ears to catch, might yet assure them that they were not wholly orphans, even though one parent should have perished. No shout was ever heard; nor could a shout in any case have been heard, for the night was one of tumultuous wind. And though, amidst its ravings, sometimes they fancied a sound of voices, still, in the dead lulls that now and then succeeded, they heard nothing to confirm their hopes.

The night slipped away and morning came, bringing with it no better hopes of any kind. Change there had been none, but for the worse: the snow had greatly increased in quantity, and the drifts seemed far more formidable. A second day passed like the first; little Agnes still keeping her young flock quiet and tolerably comfortable.

A third day came; and there came a welcome gleam of hope. The arrangement of the snow-drifts had shifted during the night; and though the wooden bridge was still impracticable, a low wall had been exposed, over which, by a circuit round the brook, it seemed possible that a road might be found into Grasmere. The little boys accompanied their sister till she came to the other side of the hill, which, lying more sheltered from the weather, offered a path onwards comparatively easy. Here they parted; and little Agnes pursued her solitary mission to the nearest house she could find accessible in Grasmere.

No house could have proved a wrong one in such a case. Horror in an instant displaced the smile of hospitable greeting, when little weeping Agnes told her sad tale. No tongue can express the fervid sympathy which travelled through the vale, like fire in an American forest, when it was learned that neither George nor Sarah Green had been seen by their children since the day of the Langdale sale.

Within half-an-hour, or little more, from the remotest parts of the valley all the men of Grasmere had assembled, and 60 at least set off with the speed of Alpine hunters to the hills. The dangers of the undertaking were considerable under the uneasy and agitated state of the weather, and all the women of the vale were in the greatest anxiety until night brought them back, in a body, unsuccessful. For three days at the least – and I rather think five – the search was ineffectual. The zeal of the people, meantime, was not in the least abated, but rather quickened, by the wearisome disappointment; every hour of daylight was turned to account, no man of the valley came home to meals.

At length sagacious dogs were taken up, and about noon day a shout from an aerial height, amongst thick volumes of cloudy vapour, propagated through repeating bands of men for a distance of many miles, conveyed as by telegraph into Grasmere the news that the bodies were found. George Green was lying at the bottom of a precipice, from which he had fallen. Sarah Green was found on the summit of the precipice. It was conjectured that the husband had desired his wife to pause for a few minutes, wrapping her meantime in his own greatcoat, whilst he should go forward and reconnoitre the ground, in order to catch a sight of some object (rocky peak, or tarn, or peat-field) which might ascertain their position. Either the snow above – already lying in drifts – or the blinding snow-storm, must have misled him as to the nature of the circumjacent ground, for the precipice over which he had fallen was but a few yards from the spot on which he had quitted his wife. ❄

The graves of George and Sarah Green can be found at St. Oswald's Church, Grasmere.

SHUGGLES, COGS & STEW: THE DIALECT OF SNEW

THE Inuit famously have dozens of words for snow – but Cumbrians can give them a good run for their money, with dialect describing a dazzling variety of the white stuff.

Broo – Snow broo, snow broth: half-melted snow.

Burr – A hazy ring around the moon before the arrival of snow.

Coald pye or **penny pye** – A fall on the ice.

Cobs, Cogs – Clumps of snow on the feet of men or horses.

Daad – A slight covering of snow, as in "A la'al daad o' snow on t' grund."

Daud – A flake of snow.

Doon-fo – Not the downfall of empires or of kings, but of soft, silent snow, as in "We're gaan to hev some doon-fo."

Dreuvy – Water that is not quite clear, especially in half-melted snow.

Drip – Driven or newly-fallen snow of exceptional white. 'White as drip' means something brilliantly white.

Drufted snow – Snow driven into drifts by the wind.

Flodder – Half-dissolved snow. There is a Dutch word, floderen, which means 'to trudge through wet and dirt'.

Flowe – Wild, bleak and cold, as in "It's flowe weather."

Flutther'd up – Of a drain: filled and choked with snow.

Frostit – Spoiled by frost.

Gildert – Snares attached to a hoop for entrapping birds in the snow.

Green Christmas – A Christmas without snow. It is said that "A green Christmas makes a fat kirk-yard".

Grimin, Greymin or **Grymin** – A sprinkling or slight covering of snow. The word seems to originate from the word grime, in its original sense of covering easily removed.

Hackt – Cracked hands from cold or neglect.

Hadder – To drizzle or 'small rain'.

Hask – Dry, cold weather.

Hisk – The difficulty a person experiences in breathing on plunging into a cold bath, as in "He hisk't when he went in."

Ice shockle or shuggle – Icicle.

Kins, Keens – Cracks in the hand caused by frost.

Knee-deep – As in "The snow is knee-deep".

Murk-drife – Snow falling during grey and overcast weather. From murke – dark, gloomy – and drife – snow blown in the wind.

Onfa – A heavy fall of snow or rain.

Overblow – Storm of drifting snow.

Overblown – When snow drifts over sheep sheltering behind a rock or wall. Sheep have been known to survive days, even weeks, under overblown snow.

Peenjan – Freezing with cold.

Plonch – The action of wading or walking, or both at once, as in "Plonchin aboot up ta yan's knees in snow broth, it's eniuf ta gie yan yan's deeth o'cauld."

Rag – Hoar frost.

Shot ice – Ice frozen on the surface of the ground.

Skoggers – Auld stocking legs, as in "Auld stocking legs tied over t' clog tops ta keep 'snow oot. An' rare an' useful they er."

Skurl – To slide on the ice in clogs.

Slush – Half-melted snow. Also slops; thin mud; snow broth; a dirty person.

Smoorin – Smothering, or covering over, as snow over ground or treacle over bread.

Snew – Snow. When snow lingers on the ground it is said 'to be waiting for more'. To 'go like snow off a ditch' is to disappear quickly. The expression is used in reference to families that have died off rapidly.

Snow wreaths – Piles of snow left in a lace-like pattern overhanging ditches.

Sno-broth – Half dissolved snow.

Starved – Frozen by cold.

Stew – Driving snow.

Stoor an drife – Small driven snow, as in "Stoor an drife fit ta blind yan."

Thow wind – Wind bringing a thaw, as in "It comes fer t' frost an' snow, an' its a snizer at times."

Whewt – A whiff of now, as in "A few whewts o' snow." ❄

PART 4

TRADITIONS

MERRY NEETS

Merry neets – or merry nights – were highlights of the social calendar in the 18th and 19th centuries. They were evenings when villagers gathered at an inn to eat, drink, dance and, if the company proved fine, 'speak the soft language of love'. The Christmas neet was particularly popular.

'Ballads in the Cumberland Dialect', Robert Anderson, 1840.

The common people in Cumberland, like the common people in all countries, have their festive scenes in which they mingle with ardour, and forget awhile the toils, cares and hardships peculiar to their stations. Amidst their coarse and homely pastimes, their hearts expand to gaiety, and receive more genuine gratification than is to be found among those splendid amusements which the rich, the idle and the dissipated have invented to diversify life and remove that tedium, languor and disquietude which oppress a heart enervated by luxury and corrupted by vice.

A Cumbrian merry night is, as its name imports, a night appropriated to mirth and festivity. It takes place at some country alehouse during the holidays of Christmas, a season in which every Cumbrian peasant refuses to be governed by the cold and niggardly maxims of economy and thrift. So that the guests might want nothing to cheer their hearts, the landlord of the house is careful to replenish his cellar with ale and spirits, as well as to provide bread and cheese, pipes and tobacco, cards and music. The young women, who are particularly fond of these diversions, and who are introduced to them by some friend, relation or lover, have pies placed before them, and that girl must be modest indeed who refuses to taste of a luxury when it is within her reach.

The company are divided into different parties according to their different propensities, and to the different amusements to which they are attached. They whose ruling passion is card-playing seat themselves in some apartment where they can obtain a comfortable fire and commodious table. The sweethearters retire to some snug, sequestered corner where – unseen by licentious eye and unheard by idle ear – they can breathe the vows and speak the soft language of love. They who are fond of dancing enjoy their diversion in the house-loft, to which they ascend by means of stone steps or a ladder. Its walls are generally very low, but, as there is no ceiling, a very tall person may stand erect under its roof. The dancers exhibit specimens of agility, rather than of skill, and though their heads have often stubborn encounters with the beams and rafters of the building, they are seldom forsaken by either their spirits or their elasticity.

The music is that of the fiddle, and, if it be not so powerful as the minstrelsy of old times – which gave motion to stocks, trees, and stones – it may be truly said of it (and which is certainly no little praise) that it gives activity, if not grace, to the unweildy limbs of a Cumbrian clown. At the conclusion of a jig, the fiddler makes his instrument squeak out two notes that say, or are understood to say: "Kiss her!" – a command which the rustic youth obeys by giving his fair partner a salute equal, as far as relates to sound, to that recorded by Shakespeare, when –

> Petruchio took the bride about the neck,
> And kiss'd her lips with such a clam'rous smack,
> That, at the parting, all the church did echo. ❄

MERRY NEET AT THE CHERRY TREE

WILLIAM Wordsworth, in his poem 'Benjamin the Waggoner', recounts the revelry of a Cumberland merry neet at The Cherry Tree – an inn that stood beside the Ambleside–Keswick road near Wythburn before the flooding of Thirlmere.

'The poetical works of William Wordsworth', William Wordsworth, 1882.

'BLITHE souls and lightsome hearts have we,
Feasting at the Cherry Tree!"
This was the outside proclamation,
This was the inside salutation;
What bustling – jostling – high and low!
A universal overflow!
What tankards foaming from the tap!
What store of cakes in every lap!
What thumping, stumping, overhead!
The thunder had not been more busy:
With such a stir you would have said,
This little place may well be dizzy!
Tis who can dance with greatest vigour –
Tis what can be most prompt and eager;
As if it heard the fiddle's call,
The pewter clatters on the wall;
The very bacon shows its feeling,
Swinging from the smoky ceiling!

BROUGH MERRY NEET

The merry night at Brough was preceded on Twelfth Night by a curious tradition of parading a burning holly bush through the streets. It continued until the closing days of the 19th century.

'The Penrith Observer', 5 January, 1875.

ON Twelfth Night at Brough, the very ancient custom of carrying the holly tree through the town is observed. There are two or three inns in the town which provide for the ceremony alternately, though the townspeople lend a hand to prepare the tree, to every branch of which a torch composed of greased rushes is affixed.

At about eight o'clock in the evening the tree is taken to a convenient part of the town, where the torches are lighted – the town band accompanying and playing till all is completed – when it is carried up and down the town, preceded by the band and crowd, who have now formed in procession.

Many of the inhabitants carry lighted branches and flambeaus*, and rockets and squibs† &c are discharged on the occasion. After the tree has been thus paraded, and the torches are nearly burnt out, it is taken to the middle of the town, where amidst the cheers and shouts of the multitude, it is thrown among them. Then begins a scene of noise and confusion, for the crowd, watching the opportunity, rush in and cling to the branches, the contention being to bear it to the rival inns, 'sides' having been formed for that purpose; the reward being an ample allowance of ale &c to the successful competitors.

The landlord derives his benefit from the numbers the victory attracts, and – the fiddler being all ready – a 'merry night' as it is called here is got up, the lads and lasses dancing away till morning.

Although the origin of this custom is lost, and no tradition exists by which it can be traced, it may not be a strained surmise to ascribe it to the church ceremonies of the day when branches of trees were carried in procession to decorate the altar in commemoration of the offering of the Magi. In Catholic countries, lights and torches always abound in their ceremonies, and persons residing in the streets through which they pass testify their zeal and piety by providing flambeaus at their own expense and bringing them lighted to the doors of their houses. ❄

* *Flambeau – A burning torch.*
† *Squib – A firework; a term still in use today – as in 'a damp squib', something of a disappointment.*

THE GRASMERE CAROL

GRASMERE is proud to have its very own Christmas carol. 'The Grasmere Carol' was composed by Windermere-born Arthur Somervell in 1924 for the Grasmere Players, the village's theatrical troupe, who continue to tread the boards for the entertainment of villagers to this day.

THE Grasmere players have long been associated with an annual performance of dialect plays. The tradition started in 1893 when Miss Charlotte Fletcher, daughter of the vicar, wrote a play called 'The Dalesman'. The performance proved hugely popular. When Miss Fletcher left the village, more dialect plays were written by Eleanor Gertrude and Catherine Simpson. Miss Simpson would go on to marry Canon Hardwicke Rawnsley, who fought to preserve the Lake District and was instrumental in establishing the National Trust. In 1915 he retired to Grasmere, living in Wordsworth's former home at Allan Bank – now a National Trust property.

It is known that Arthur Somervell visited the Rawnsleys, and it's almost certain that 'The Grasmere Carol' – written by Somervell as a thank-you to the Players for their efforts in preserving rural tradition – would have been sung at Allan Bank. ☛

'THE GRASMERE CAROL'
ARTHUR SOMERVELL

When Mary on that Christmas Day
Had laid her baby in the hay,
Within her heart then rang this lay,
Noël, Noël, Noël.

The oxen with no gift to bring
Stood large and silent in a ring
And wonder'd at the tiny thing
Noël, Noël, Noël.

Three kings that journey'd from afar,
Caspar, Melchior, Baldazzar,
Follow'd in faith a shining star,
Noël, Noël, Noël.

The shepherds in the field that night
Awaken'd by a sudden light
Saw overheard a wondrous sight
Noël, Noël, Noël.

With silver trumpets rais'd on high,
Bright angels stood up on the sky
While earth took up the glad reply
Noël, Noël, Noël.

They sang that little baby's birth
With hymns of joy and heavenly mirth,
"Glory to God and peace on earth,"
Noël, Noël, Noël.

Now while the starry welkin' rings
Let us arise as if on wings,
And join the shepherds and the kings
Noël, Noël, Noël.

Then in the stable rude and small
On bended knees we silent fall,
And worship at the humble stall,
Noël, Noël, Noël,
Noël, Noël, Noël.

DOWN T' LONNIN

IT is unclear who composed this charming ballad, but it was probably the late Joyce Withers, a resident of Grasmere who read 'Down t' Lonnin' for many years at the annual Christmas Readings, still held in the village. The words set the story of Mary and Joseph in Grasmere.

Read most years at the Grasmere Christmas Readings.

Down t' lonnin' they came,
Just Braithwaite's Mary with Joe,
That she wed Lammas year,
And their li'le lad in her arm.
Moon was low and clear
Above Silver How, and mists writhin' up from t' lake,
And light sharp and silver, as 'tis
Of a winter dusk with the night beginning to break
On the darkening dale.

There were no mysteries
Round Mary and Joe;
They smiled at us, going by –
"Grand evening!" Joe called out, and postie said "Aye!"
And our Libby, she ran to set them a bit on road,
As Mary turned, and showed
T' bairn sleeping soft and warm...

Up Huntingstile* they went;
And the young moon dropped over Silver How
And the night shut down; and now
We saw them no more;

Their footsteps after a while
Died into mists and darkness.

Up lonnin'† they came
Late in the evenin';
We never heard them come,
Though night was still
As a sheltered tarn is – only a whisper from
The li'le beck near at hand,
Splashin' down in spate.

Quiet they came, and late,
And none said owt as they passed us – just so
A young lass, walking wearily, and a man
...like Joe... Or not so like, maybe?
...and the two of 'em bent
Over a bairn asleep; and as they went
Through the dark trees and lake mists,
There was light.

Up lonnin' they came,
Just Braithwaite's lass wi' her man,
On a winter's night –
Just Braithwaite's Mary – who else?
In the Christmas night.

* *Huntingstile is just south of Grasmere village. It leads to a path that crosses the fell to Chapel Stile.*

† *Lonning – A country lane, usually low-level and about half-a-mile long. Lonnings often lead to a farm and the term may have originated as the path to the 'loan' – 'the quiet place by the farm', where people could buy milk, eggs or other farm produce.*

TAR BARRELS

CUMBRIAN Christmas traditions come and go – but carrying burning tar barrels down the high street is probably one most folk are glad to have seen consigned to history.

UNTIL the early part of the 19th Century it was the tradition in Workington, and other parts of Cumberland, to carry old tar barrels down the streets as part of the town's Christmas celebrations. These barrels were set alight, and when the person carrying the barrel could bear the heat no longer, he'd drop it, with the perhaps predictable consequence that it would roll into a shop doorway and set the building ablaze. As a consequence, in 1840 the town's authorities issued an order banning the practice. They also took the opportunity to ban football, throwing snowballs and any game that might cause annoyance to residents. Here is how *The Pacquet* reported on the 'Silent Night' outcome of the order:

'The Cumberland Pacquet', 29 December, 1840.

We are glad to learn that the authorities in Workington have put an end to the foolish and highly dangerous practice of carrying lighted tar-barrels through the streets of that town on Christmas Eve. The precautionary measures of the Trustees and the vigilance of the police on that evening effectually prevented the unmeaning but dangerous exhibition which for years past has been witnessed in the town. Hence Workington on Christmas Eve last, which used to be the scene of tumult and disorder, not unaccompanied with danger, was as quiet and peaceable as any place within her Majesty's dominions. ❄

BARRING-OUT

IF anyone thinks school discipline these days is 'not like it was in the old days', they might read their history books and note the mischief of pupils past. A Christmas custom in which schoolboys and girls barricaded the school in a stand-off with teachers has long since died out, but in the early days of the 19th century the tradition became so boisterous it frequently ended with pupils or teachers being injured.

'Old Yarns of English Lakeland', W. T. Palmer, 1914.

SOON after the master had gone to dinner, the door was bolted and locked – and how tardy was his return! At five minutes to one he would stroll into the school yard, look amazed at its unwonted quietude, and, still puzzling, stop to draw out his big watch with gold seals. Having leisurely consulted this, he came up to the school door and tried the sneck*. A pen handle or a slate pencil had secured this, and the old man tried again. Inside the school was silence, broken only by the nervous tittering of the girls and maybe the suppressed sobs of the scared 'babies'.

"Open that door at once," called the master, "I know you aren't all truanting." There was no reply – there was a stringent code in regard to this, and the old man knew it well.

"James Thompson, open that door or I'll warm you." Still no reply.

"What do you want by fastening the school door? I'll stick the lot of you, and give you double tasks."

Now was the time to chant our chorus: "Six weeks' holiday and no tasks," – at which the old man simulated much fury.

"I'll give you no holidays at all, and double tasks if you don't open that door at once."

Again we chorused our demands: "Let me in, and I'll see about it." But the door was held.

"I'll give you a week's holiday if you'll be good lads and lasses," was equally scorned as a concession.

"If you don't open that door, I'll bring some of your fathers to see what bad lads you are."

Yet still we kept the door locked, and at length the old man, threatening unutterable things, went off to bring a choice selection of fathers to wallop us into obedience.

His retirement was the signal for our next action: across the big meadow was a wood, and the time-honoured ritual of 'barring-out' now demanded that we should break bounds for this cover, once within which it was hopeless for the schoolmaster to recapture us.

So out in due time we sallied, every big one dragging a little boy or girl as fast as their little legs could go. If the master caught any of us before the wood was reached, then the holiday was forfeit. And sure enough there he is in pursuit – run, run... For his threat to bring down parental wrath was merely a ruse, and he has got into the school by the back door, only waited to snatch up his stick, and is coming fast. Woe fare the boy that is captured, for, after the schoolmaster has finished with him, we will all and several give him a good hiding for his laziness. Girls don't count.

But ah! One remembers that the schoolmaster reckoned his distance and pace so well that none were captured – though it might be that some terrified 'infant' had tripped in the hay and lay there, howling terribly. If such a disaster occurred, the old man was equal to the occasion: "Never mind, Jimmy, it's only the big lads I'm after. I'll warm them." By the time he reached the edge of the wood, his little flock was scattered far and wide therein, singing joyfully: "Four weeks' holiday and no tasks," for to that our demand had been whittled down.

After a while the old man marched back to the school, and, standing on the doorstep, produced the whistle which was our usual call to assembly, and, knowing that victory was ours, there was an answering stampede schoolwards. The old man was at his desk, and as soon as the shuffling and seating was over he announced that the school would be closed for four weeks and that we could go at once... no mention of tasks anywhere! Hip-pip-hooray!, as we vulgar little boys would have it.

EVIDENCE of how out-of-control 'barring-out' became is provided by the 1702 rules of Carlisle Grammar School, which finally ended the tradition – and in particular the use of swords and pistols by the students – replacing it with a more orderly 'performance of exercise'. *Boring!*

Statute order no. 29: That the rude and barbarous usage of barring-out the Master and taking violent possession of the school, and coming armed with swords and pistols, shooting with guns and pistols, be abolished and layd aside. And that instead of it, there be a performance of exercise and orderly entertainment, and collation, for the masters and strangers, gentlemen of the city (and the Dean and Chapter, Mayor and Aldermen, if they come as formerly they have done) in token of their grateful sense of their master's favour in granting them a vacation and remission from studies. ❄

* *Sneck – The latch of a door or gate.*

RUM BUTTER

CUMBRIAN families still partake of rum butter at Christmas. It's a local delicacy held in high esteem, and every family has its own theory as to where the concoction originated.

RUM butter is a traditional delicacy still eaten by Cumbrians at Christmas and at special occasions such as weddings and christenings. Many families still have a 'rum butter bowl' from which it should be served. There are two recipes – one for the old county of Westmorland, and one for Cumberland (the two counties merged in 1974 to form Cumbria); the only difference is that the butter is melted on the stove in the Cumberland recipe, but blended unmelted in the Westmorland one.

There are a number of theories-cum-legends that explain how rum butter originated. This unsigned and undated document held by Whitehaven Archive and Record Office offers one...

Unsourced document, Whitehaven Archive and Local Studies Centre.

A TINY village in the early 17th century, Whitehaven grew dramatically to become a major British seaport by the middle of the 18th century. Although its trade was predominantly that of supplying coal to Ireland, strong links were forged with many parts of the world. Tobacco, sugar and spirits, for example, were imported from American and the West Indies, and these commodities were stored in various bonded warehouses in the town.

Alongside this legitimate trade, smuggling flourished on a large scale, and there is a strong tradition that Cumberland rum butter was originally concocted by local smugglers in the 18th century.

One misty morning at very low tide, a smuggling vessel called the Sea Witch captained by Moses Kennedy unloaded a consignment of goods near the village of Parton. As some of the men came ashore they realised that they had been observed by customs men and took refuge in a cave, taking their booty with them. As the tide came in, the mouth of the cave was submerged, and the customs men belied that the smugglers would be drowned. For days, guards stood watch, expecting to see the bodies of the smugglers emerge from the cave. Eventually it was assumed that the men were dead, and the officers withdrew.

During this time, however, the smugglers were quite safe, as the cave possessed an upper level beyond the reach of water. Amongst their goods were three edible items: rum, butter and sugar. These they mixed together into a paste, which sustained them for the duration of their confinement, said to be about a fortnight!

The legend may well be based on an actual incident, but whatever the truth of the matter, rum butter almost certainly originated in the area. To this day, local christening celebrations traditionally include the serving of rum butter to symbolise survival. It is, of course, considered more prestigious if Whitehaven rum butter is served in an antique dish made many years ago at one of the Whitehaven potteries*. ☞

* *For many years, Whitehaven was famous for its potteries.*

A RECIPE FOR RUM BUTTER

Traditionally served on cream crackers, rum butter also tastes delicious on toast, scones, fresh bread and teacakes. It can be used as an alternative to brandy butter on Christmas pudding.

RUM BUTTER INGREDIENTS

- 1lb soft brown sugar.
- ½lb butter.
- Slosh of dark rum (Jefferson's for preference).
- Pinch of spice: nutmeg, cinnamon, or both.

RECIPE

- Put the butter in a heat-proof bowl over a saucepan of near-boiling water so the steam softens the butter.
- Stir in the sugar until it melts into the butter.
- Add the rum and spice, stir vigorously then pour into a bowl.
- Allow to cool and set before serving.

– You can cheat and use a microwave – but be careful not to burn the butter.

– Recipe courtesy of Margaret Crosby.

POWSOWDY

WARM ale and bread are the basis for this unlikely sounding traditional Christmas delicacy.

POWSOWDY is a Cumbrian delicacy so wrapped in mystery that even the spelling of its name varies wildly. Sometimes it's powsoddy and sometimes it's powsoddie, powsondie or any other combination of those letters. Many today define it as small pieces of bread dipped in warm ale (with rum being added in some parts of the county), but recipes are as varied as its spelling. The Scots have their own variants too, typically adding a sheep's head to the broth.

What *is* known is that the concoction dates back at least 200 years and was traditionally eaten (or drunk, depending on its viscosity) around Christmas time. In fact, the villages of Westmorland celebrated Powsowdy Night on Candlemas (2 February) in the 19th century. To confuse things even more, some believe the food/drink was a relic of the Roman festival Lupercalia, which roughly equates with our Valentine's Day.

The village of Lamplugh claims powsowdy as its own, referring to it as Lamplugh Pudding. Some believe it originated as a pudding used by shepherds when they were out in winter looking for sheep on the snow-riven fells. But another story tells how a Lamplugh woman was snow-bound in her cottage for days and she took the only ingredients she had in her kitchen to concoct a meal to keep her fed and warm: the result was Lamplugh pudding.

Helen Shipton-Smith grew up in west Cumbria and now runs Helens Herbs (helensherbs.co.uk).

Here she gives the traditional pudding a sweet and herby twist:

POWSOWDY INGREDIENTS

Makes four servings.

- ½ pint Newcastle Brown Ale.
- 1 teaspoon cinnamon.
- Ground cloves.
- Juice of ½ a lemon.
- 56g demerara sugar.
- 40g porridge oats.
- Chocolate chip cookies, crushed.

RECIPE

- Pour the ale into a saucepan and add the cinnamon, a sprinkle of ground cloves and the lemon juice.
- Gently mix the ingredients over a medium heat.
- Add the demerara sugar and porridge oats and allow the powsowdy to thicken.
- Let it cool, then crush and sprinkle over the chocolate chip cookies to decorate.

THE KISSING BUSH

AN early 20th century Christmas tradition in many Cumbrian households was a hanging decoration called the 'kissing bush'. This typically consisted of two large hoops decorated with crêpe paper and baubles – the structure then being hung from the ceiling. Below are the memories of Jim Park, 92, of Christmases and kissing bushes during his Whitehaven childhood in the 1930s.

THE kissing bush was hung from the centre of the room – this was the days before the electric light, so you didn't have any light fittings to worry about. We usually made the kissing bush about four days before Christmas, and you had to have it down by 6 January, Twelfth Night. We also decorated the room with paper chains and a peacock decoration was hung from the bottom of the bush; this had belonged to my grandmother. Mistletoe was hung from the bottom of the kissing bush for people to kiss under, but mistletoe was hung all over the house for this purpose*.

We didn't have a Christmas tree – the kissing bush was instead of a tree – but many of our neighbours had trees instead of kissing bushes. I went to St. James School in Whitehaven. Each year one of the local primary schools would hold a nativity and the other schools attended in turn.

We went carol singing each year around the streets of Whitehaven. There were about 30 of us – men, women, boys and girls – but we weren't in the church choir; these were all people from the Orange Lodge†, which was strong in Whitehaven at that time. There was one old lady at the top of Queen Street who would invite us all in and give everyone a drink.

I would write a letter to Father Christmas each year and it was then thrown in the fire – I was told that the smoke would send the message up to Father Christmas. The presents were left at the end of our beds for us to find in the morning and there was one present we got every year: a fort and some soldiers! Each year the fort would disappear a few weeks before Christmas and we would then receive it back again on Christmas morning… freshly painted. We would also have a sock hung from the mantelpiece over the fire filled with apples, oranges and pomegranates.

On Christmas morning we had to go to church at 11am (this was Trinity Church in Whitehaven, which no longer exists). There were no decorations in the church, but there were flowers in a holder on the end of each pew. Our Christmas dinner was at lunchtime. We couldn't afford a turkey, but we had a big chicken. The Christmas pudding contained silver three-penny bits, but when the three-penny bit was changed into the larger coin, six-pences were used instead. We also had a box of Christmas crackers each year, which mum bought from the butchers. In the afternoon, relatives would visit – dad had two sisters and a brother – but these were just flying visits in which they left a present. We would also play games in the afternoon, including Ludo and dominoes.

On Boxing Day people would go on a good long walk – we would go down to the North Pier on Whitehaven harbour. ☛

The custom of making a kissing bush at Christmas has all but died out in Cumbria. A few families still maintain the tradition and, in hopes of a revival, here's how to make one...

Instructions for making a kissing bush

1. Tie two wire or plastic hoops, around 12in to 15in in diameter, together at 90 degrees angles. Secure them firmly.
2. Pad the hoops with insulating tubing or old newspapers. Tubing is better, because you can pin decorations to it.
3. Get some crêpe paper and cut it into strips. Fold the paper in half lengthwise and make a cut about ¾ of the width at about half to one inch intervals.
4. Fold the crêpe paper back on itself and the loops will spring out to make the 'leaves' of the bush.
5. Glue one of the crêpe lengths at the top of the hoop and wrap it around the hoop. Continue until all the hoop is covered with crêpe paper.
6. Decorate the rest of the bush with Christmas decorations.
7. Hang the kissing bush from the ceiling. ❄

** Jim does not know the origins of the name 'kissing bush', but does not think it came from the tradition of kissing under the mistletoe.*

† The Loyal Orange Institution, commonly known as the Orange Order, is an international protestant fraternal order based in Northern Ireland but with lodges in England and Scotland. It was once strong in west Cumbria.

THE CUSHION DANCE

Alexander Craig Gibson wrote in 1870 about a 'cushion dance' that traditionally ended merry neet celebrations. We reprint the instructions here for those brave enough to try it...

'Folk-Speech of Cumberland', Alexander Craig Gibson, 1869.

A young man carrying a cushion paces round the room in time to the appropriate tune, selects a girl, lays the cushion at her feet, and both kneel upon it and kiss, the fiddler making an extraordinary squeal during the operation. The girl then takes the cushion to another young man, who kisses her as before, and leaves her free to 'link' with the first, and march round the room. This is repeated till the whole party is brought in, when they all form a circle, and 'kiss out' in the same manner, sometimes varying it by the kissers sitting on two chairs, back to back, in the middle of the ring, and kissing over their shoulders – a trying process to bashful youth of either sex.

THE MUMMERS

MUMMERS would perform each Christmas at local manor houses, at pubs or even on street corners. Their curious plays – featuring a battle between hero and villain – were comic nonsense, but they had roots in medieval times. In some corners of Cumbria mummer enthusiasts continue to perform today.

MUMMERS plays are still performed at many villages throughout England. The St Bees mummers on the west coast of Cumbria tour village pubs each Christmas Eve with a play known to have been performed in the area around St Bees and Whitehaven for nearly two centuries.

Mummers have been likened to winter-time morris men, and it is often the local morris side that keeps the tradition going. They enter the pub or village hall and perform a short 'play' that features an array of stock characters such as St George, Beelzebub and the King of Egypt. A typical mummers' plot centres on a battle between hero and villain (in the St Bees play, the hero is Prince George and the villain Alexander). The hero is mortally wounded, but a quack doctor miraculously restores him to life so that he can fight the villain once more – and this time defeat him.

The origin of mummers plays is unknown, but they are found all over Europe and America, taken over by British colonists. Frequent references to the Holy Land and Jerusalem suggest they originated during the Crusades. Many of the plays also mention mince pies – a delicacy with ingredients that can also be traced back to the Holy Land. The death and rebirth of the hero echoes many mid-winter traditions, which symbolise the death of the old year and birth of the new. Saying anything more certain about the plays' origins is no more than supposition. Today the plays are a bit of nonsense, carried out by enthusiasts and usually raising money for charity – but they're also keeping an ancient tradition alive.

What follows is an extract from the Whitehaven mummers play, 'Alexander and The King of Egypt', performed by the St Bees Mummers to raise money for the lifeboat charity, the RNLI.

Prince George:
I am Prince George, a champion brave and bold,
For with my spear I have won three crowns of gold,
'Twas I that brought the dragon to the slaughter,
And I that gained the Egyptian Monarch's daughter.

Alex:
Hold, Slasher, hold, pray do not be so hot,
For in this place thou knowest not who thou'st got.
'Tis I that's to hash and smash thee as small as flies,
And send thee to Satan to make mince pies,
Mince pies hot, mince pies cold,
I'll send thee to Satan ere three days are told.

Alexander and Prince George fight; the latter is wounded and falls.

King of Egypt:
Is there never a doctor to be found
That can cure my son of his deadly wound?

Doctor:
Yes, there is a doctor to be found,
That can cure your son of his deadly wound.

King of Egypt:
What disease can he cure?

Doctor:
All diseases, both within and out,
Broken legs, heads, arms, and the gout;
To cure your son, good sir, I fear not,
With this small bottle which by me I've got.
The balsam is the best it does contain,
Rise up, my good Prince George and fight again.

Prince George is miraculously cured.

Prince George:
Bouncer, Buckler, mummers dear,
And Christmas comes but once a year,
Though when it comes it brings good cheer,
So farewell, Christmas, once a year.
Farewell, adieu, we wish friendship and unity,
I hope we have made sport and pleased the company;
But gentlemen, you see, we are but actors four
We've done our best, and the best can do no more.

Enter Beelzebub.

Beelzebub:
Here comes I that never come yet,
Big head and little wit,
Let my wit be ever so small,

I'll act my part amongst you all,
My name's Old Harry Sloan, that everybody knows
They put me in cornfields to fly away the crows
I went to the miller's to buy a sack of flour
I came to a ditch and I couldn't get o'er.
I saddled my horse and I drew my sword
And down I fell upon the high road.
Some say the king's dead, and buried in a saucer,
Some say he's up again and gone to be a grocer.
I went to my aunt Betty's to get some bread and butter
And being in a hurry I fell into a gutter.
Here comes I old Beelzebub,
Over my shoulder I carry a club
In my hand my frying pan
Now, don't you think I'm a jolly old man?
Money I want, and money I crave,
If you don't give me money, I'll sweep you all to your grave. ❄

A DAUGHTER WRITES HOME

A mummers performance was witnessed by Dora Harcourt in 1821 while staying with relatives at The Friars, a farmhouse outside Whitehaven. She wrote to her father in London telling him about the tradition and other Christmas customs she saw in coastal Cumberland.

The letters of Dora Harcourt, 'The Illustrated Magazine of Art', 1853.

MY Dear Father – May the bright sunshine of this splendid morning be an auspicious omen that a happy and prosperous new year awaits you.

On the eve of the 25th, a party of mummers dressed in most fantastic costume came to The Friars, and were admitted into the hall, where we saw them enact St George and the Dragon with great spirit; though one of the Armstrongs, who played the part of the King of Egypt, could not restrain his laughing propensities and in the midst of a solemn charge to the doctor on doing his duty burst into a loud guffaw that proved highly infectious to most present – while it scandalised old Sally to the last degree. She even carried her resentment so far as to present the luckless wight, when the play was ended, with a bowl of hot buttermilk instead of the hot ale that had been prepared for the players; but my uncle took care that every mummer should receive an ample dole of meat, bread and wassail* piping hot, and half-a-crown to boot, so all withdrew very pleased.

They were succeeded by a droll set of very young boys and girls, who, in shrill childish treble, shouted rather than sang some old rhymes, commencing: "Ule, ule, ule, three puddings in a pule". They, too, were allowed to come into the hall, and were then persuaded to sing one or two carols more gently, and consequently more pleasingly. Sally brought them some milk, but on my uncle's insisting that the half-starved urchins should partake of the ale, a large old-fashioned silver tankard was produced, furnished with pegs stuck in at regular intervals. Each child was made to drink what filled the space between two of the pegs, and I was made to comprehend the literal meaning of one's spirits being a peg too low.

A plate heaped up with narrow but substantial mince pies, baked in the form of a horse's manger in commemoration of advent, was next handed round, and the happy little ones went forth again into the freezing atmosphere.

At breakfast on Christmas Day we were each complimented by the gift of a dough image, meant to represent the Virgin's holy infant, which had been sent by the chief baker in Whitehaven. The day was brilliantly cold, and the evergreens – glittering in the most exquisite frost-work embroidery – seemed to invite one to go out and enjoy the clear, bracing air, and wander forth amidst the white sparkling fairyland around us. We accordingly set off for church half-an-hour before the usual time, and thus came in for the droll spectacle of a country wedding, Christmas Day being a favourite for the purpose.

On arriving at the church, we found it occupied by the village schoolboys, who have from time immemorial been privileged to levy a monied tax upon all bridal assemblages, which goes to the fund for supplying coals for the schoolroom fire. We were looking at the beautiful decorations of the interior of the church, formed by wreaths of evergreens and magnificent branches of yew, holly, box and ivy, which custom Robert told me had been employed even in apostolic times as a token that our Saviour was born at the Jewish Feast of Tabernacles, thus marking the season of the year in which the advent took place, when a cry from the village lads of "They're coming!" sent us to the entrance door.

Picture to yourself a motley assemblage of men and women all mounted on horses of every description, racing in the utmost confusion at the fastest speed towards the church. An elderly spinster reached it first, and very proud she seemed. I could scarcely believe this was really the expected wedding party, nor that they had ridden thus, starting from the bride's house, at least six miles. My aunt said they were indebted to the frost for their unusual exemption from the mud, which generally bespatters alike both men and women on each occasion.

On leaving the church the bridegroom gave six-pence to the delegated scholars, who held a plate at the door, and everyone who wore boots and spurs was obliged to follow his example; those who could only boast of boots minus spurs were let off with the payment of three-pence. The bridal party then re-mounted their steeds and rode off again, pausing, however, a few minutes on the brow of an adjoining eminence to listen to a congratulatory poem, recited in a loud yet snuffling voice by the head boy of the school, which was rewarded by a donation that went towards the book fund.

Of the fun we had that same evening, I have already written to you, and, indeed the amusements of snap-dragon†, dancing, yule-log and banqueting are too well-known, even in London, to need detailing. The only novel features in the evening scene were the pleasant admixture of rich and poor gathered together under my uncle's hospitable roof, and the importance which appeared to be universally attached to the foretelling of one's fortune in divers mystical ways.

I was yesterday interrupted in my letter by a call from the young couple whose wedding we witnessed on Christmas Day. They came to beg a little corn, and were making a round of calls on their friends and neighbours, who had each given them a small quantity. These donations would set them up in seed for their first crop. This custom is called 'corn laiting'. I shall hardly, I suppose, undergo this ceremonial, but the writing about it has brought the future before me so strongly that I feel little inclination to continue my descriptions; besides, next week I shall be once more at home, when we can talk over fully all I have heard and seen since I came here.

Yet, six months hence, if you will condescend to visit the Cumberland mountains, very proud, indeed, will you make your truly affectionate daughter. ❄

* *Wassail – Mulled wine or spiced ale.*

† *Snap-dragon – A game played by covering raisins in brandy and setting light to them; you then had to try and eat them.*

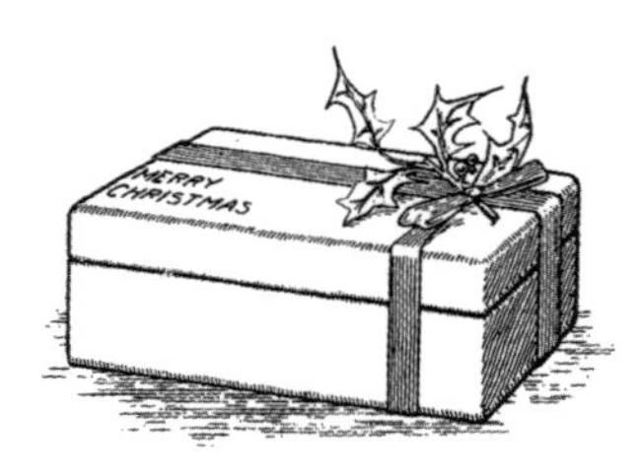

THE END OF CHRISTMAS BOXES

IT was once common custom for grocers to reward loyal customers with an annual 'Christmas box' – a few trifles to say thank-you for the year's patronage. By the early years of the 20th century the practice was dying out – and quite right, too, according to this leader writer from the *Wigton Advertiser.*

'Wigton Advertiser', 24 October, 1903.

WE shall soon be thinking about Christmas, of which the appearance of 'Annuals' and special supplement pictures on the bookstalls is already prophetic. In connection with the coming festive season, we note that there is a combination amongst grocers against what is styled the 'pernicious system of giving presents at Christmas'.

Last year a large number of shop-keepers refrained from presenting their customers with Christmas boxes. The grocer is practically the only tradesman who is called upon to give his customers rewards for their patronage. This year, however, the grocer has in most cases set his face against such a drain upon his profits: no Christmas box need be expected from him.

There is no reason why a man should give us something for the privilege of supplying our needs, unless, indeed, he is able by overcharge to recoup himself for the outlay occasion by the provisions of the so-called presents... The public should be astute enough to recognise that persons do not embark in business for the purpose of giving something for nothing... ❄

THE SCHOOL NATIVITY

'The Whitehaven News', 5 January, 1978.

A WORKINGTON Infant School was in uproar when the second of the three Wise Men delivered a line that was new to most Nativity scripts. The first Wise Man bent over the baby Jesus: "I bring you a gift of gold". The second Wise Man, however, forgot his lines. As his face reddened, the toddler had the place in hysterics as he uttered the immortal line: "Oh aye, Frank sent this."

SILENT NIGHT (PLEASE)

THE angelic voices of children singing carols in the street is enough to melt even the iciest of winter hearts. Not so for this epistle writer from Carlisle...

'Carlisle Gazette', 27 December, 1910.

THE newspapers have lately contained 'seasonable' articles on Christmas customs, carols, yule logs and the like. I do not propose to say much on the subject, but I cannot refrain from commenting on the indiscriminate nature of much of the 'carolling' which is going on while I write these lines. Passing the other night by the house of an aged spinster, I was amused to hear children gathered round the door singing:

God bless the master of this house,
Likewise the mistress too,
And all the little children
Around the table too.

Little did the youngsters dream that the doggerel they were so persistently chanting was little less than an insult to the inmate of the house, which never in living memory had either a master or contained a little child. The cheerful nature, however, of the singers, no doubt took the sting away, and even now while penning these lines, voices at the door have treated me to an indiscriminate hash made up of 'The Lassie From Lancashire', 'Hark the Herald' and 'Lead, Kindly Light'. *– Borderer.*

CHRISTMAS IN THE YEAR 2000

The refrain of 'Auld Lang Syne' – recorded in Cumbria for centuries, and still sung today – looks back at past times. But what of the ghosts of Christmas *future*? In this prescient piece written for *The Whitehaven News* in 1967, contributor Carole Lawrence evokes a future of 'TVs no larger than transistor radios' and 'high streets turned into warehouses'.

'The Whitehaven News', 7 December, 1967.

CHRISTMAS in the Big Brother world of George Orwell did not exist at all; Santa Claus was dead. Indeed, he had never lived. Many eminent sociologists are today profoundly pessimistic at a rate of social progress which is carrying mankind swiftly, it seems, towards Big Brother living. But to take the optimistic view that 2000 will be just as much a Christian celebration as now leads to interesting speculation. Firstly Christmas Day 2000 will be the greatest festival ever known simply because of the anniversary.

On Christmas Day 2000 greetings will be sent around the world in colour by television, person to person, as simply as a telegram. There will be two TV systems in every home: one for news and entertainment, the other for personal use, linked to telephone networks. Thus Mr Smith in Hong Kong will dial his home in London from his hotel room, say "Happy Christmas" and watch his children open their presents.

What will be in those bright bulky packages only Father Christmas knows? He will have had a staggering variety of gifts to choose from. More popular than today, probably, will be travel vouchers – tickets for supersonic weekend tours of, say, Kenya or Brazil – anywhere where wild animals and vegetations are still free and unchecked. A ticket to Tokyo from London will cost about £50 in the new world currency. £50 will represent perhaps one week's pay for a medium-grade computer operator.

Very young children will find midget colour TV sets, no larger than today's transistor radios, in their Christmas stockings, and tiny wire recorders. Toys will probably be of the do-it-yourself variety – built go-karts powered by selenium cells and kits for making computers and personal radars (of the type cheats will use in blind man's buff).

Teenagers will get jet-bikes, two-seater hovercraft, and electronic organs the size of a small desk that will compose pop tunes as well as play them.

Mother might prefer a second or third car – one with colour panels that can be changed to suit her mood or dress – or, if she hasn't already got one, a robot maid installed in her kitchen which will order food, store it, make up menus, cook the food and deliver it on time, as well as 'wash' fabrics with sound waves, dispose of disposable crockery, operate the automatic dust and dirt removers, and maintain the house at exactly the same temperature all year round. She might, if the family is rich enough to own a tiny plot of land (probably on the north African coast), get a second plastic home for holidays.

Five out of ten fathers, at least, will be thought by their families to already 'have everything', so Christmas presents will need to be exotic: a sub-aqua sphere for investigating the seabed in the Mediterranean; a sporting ray-gun for seal hunting in the Arctic preserves (the Arctic will be the new Safari hunting grounds); a booking for an orbital observation flight of the moon. There will be lasers for the home workshop, metal-detectors for those with the hobby of archaeology and mineralogy, and electron microscopes for amateur scientists.

Christmas decorations in both home and shops will be more mobile than the present static displays. New materials already developed but not yet a commercial proposition will produce strange effects: walls will glow with light, changing colour almost imperceptibly.

The great store windows of Oxford Street may have disappeared – space will be too valuable in stores, which will resemble automated warehouses. Other shops will be located deep underground, perhaps eight or ten floors down, with air-conditioning from midday sunshine. Many homes will be similarly hermetically sealed, without windows at all – no chimney for Santa Claus, whose only entry could be through an air-conditioning grill.

The most extraordinary Christmas in the year 2000 will without doubt be the one spent by groups of men on the moon – scientists and astronauts of maybe several nations, carried there in American and Russian rockets, establishing the possibility of using the moon as a launch pad for further exploration.

They will be digging for minerals, looking at planets and earth through electronic telescopes so high powered they will be able to pick out the village of Bethlehem. Their Christmas dinner will be from tubes and pill bottles, and it is extremely unlikely that any alcohol will be allowed – or an after-dinner cigar. Science will no doubt be tempered with sentiment, as everyone engaged on the moon research projects in America and Russia – and in the communications stations right round the world – will make every effort to bring the explorers into the earth's family circle through radio and television.

It might be that by 2000 so many men will be on the moon that a padre will be included in a rocket crew. To his unique service of thanksgiving on that morning, there might come the cosmonauts. Or they might not.

Down on earth, religious celebrations will continue as they have done for the previous 2,000 years, but in many cities the churches themselves will have changed; the new buildings will be of strange shapes and design – more functional, perhaps, than inspirational, and hundreds of them will be interdenominational, a practising symbol of ecumenicalism.

One re-enactment of history will surely be played out, and it will have deep significance to millions: hovering satellites, orbiting at the same speed as the earth's rotation, will be placed at will, dotted around the sky to relay radio waves. They will, if necessary or desirable, be visible, perhaps even in daylight.

Thus man at last will be able to plant a star and set it above the birthplace of Jesus. To half the world at least, it will be an act of dedication.

The US and Russia will be co-operating in every sphere of space and space communications, probably launching, operating and tracking each other's communications satellites for a worldwide relay network in which perhaps every country in the world will participate.

It will be irony indeed then, if that first man-made star above Bethlehem should come from the East.

If it does, perhaps the dream of peace on earth will actually have come true. ❄

A CHRISTMAS TOAST

The following toast – typical of the kind of pre-feasting speech given in the old county of Cumberland – was given at an entertainment on Christmas Day, 1858, to the villagers of Crosby Ravensworth by their vicar.

'Legends of Westmorland and Other Poems With Notes by Anthony Whitehead', 1896.

May sorrow's wings an' tail be clip,
If she attempt to flee
Ower t'boundary mark that guards the heart
Of them sea kind an free;
An may their keayle-pot nivver swing
Dry-bag'd ower the crain,
But be weel cram'd wi' beef and broth
When Christmas comes again;
Ah may we aw wi' thankful hearts
Enjoy the bounteous cheer,
An wish the generous soul that gev't
Another happy year.

CURSENMAS DIALECT

ALTHOUGH now only practised by a dedicated band of followers, Cumbrian dialect is steeped in heritage. Here's a seasonal selection box of the old tongue...

Beet – To kindle a fire.

Cald – Cold.

Christmas cannel – A candle given by grocers to each customer as a gift at Christmas.

Cock-a-lilty – In a merry mood.

Cow t'lowe – To snuff out a candle.

Cursenmas, **Cursmars**, **Kersenmas** – Christmas.

Eldin – Fuel for the fire (peat, turf or wood).

Frummerty – Wheat boiled in milk; a winter drink.

Gally-bawk – A beam or bar across the chimney, from which the pot-hooks are suspended.

Geal – To ache or tingle with cold.

Glisk – To glisten.

Goister – A loud roisterer; someone who engages in merry-making.

Goodies – Sugar sweetmeats for children.

Gox – Goose.

Grimin – A light covering of snow.

Hansel – A gift, money.

Ingle – Fireplace.

Ime or **Imin** – Short, sharp frost; hoar-frost.

Kist – A chest or trunk.

Loom – A chimney.

Owmas – Gift to a begger.

Powsoddy – A soup, hodge-podge or porridge, often involving milk, bread and other foodstuffs.

Skirl – To slide on the ice.

Storken – To freeze.

Wreeth – Snow rolled up.

Winter-proud – When wheat grows too quickly in winter.

Yule log – A large log, typically placed on the fire on Christmas Eve.